The Wandsworth Companion

The
Wandsworth
Companion

Rod Gilmour

First published 2009

The History Press
The Mill, Brimscombe Port
Stroud, Gloucestershire, GL5 2QG
www.thehistorypress.co.uk

© Rod Gilmour, 2009

The right of Rod Gilmour to be identified as the Author
of this work has been asserted in accordance with the
Copyrights, Designs and Patents Act 1988.

British Library Cataloguing in Publication Data.
A catalogue record for this book is available from the British Library.

ISBN 978 0 7524 5244 9

Typesetting and origination by The History Press
Printed in Great Britain

Contents

For Stef and Martha.

Acknowledgements

Thanks to:

Battersea Reference Library, Wandsworth Council, all at The History Press for their guidance, and the friends I have tested with facts, and subsequently bored (I know you love it really).

Image credits:

Jane's London, Miklos Kiss, Ronnie Hackston, Martin Lukashenka, Arjo Vanderjagt and Ralph Rayner and Ben Jones.

Front cover design:

Ed Way (www.spraydesigns.co.uk).

Back cover image:

Ralph Rayner.

For more information visit:

www.wandsworthcompanion.com
www.gilmourmedia.com

Introduction

Horse and carriages sauntering along Clapham Northside in Victorian times. The common bandstands. A typical working day working in the plethora of mills on the River Wandle. The borough's spirit during the Blitz. Friday nights at the splendour of Wandsworth's picture houses.

Do you ever think about what kind of place Wandsworth might once have been like? How certain places once stood? The street where you live?

Those were the thoughts and questions that started this miscellany. It started off with a variety of facts gathered over the years of living in the borough, and ended up with research missions across Wandsworth, endless hours in Battersea's historical reference library and boring my wife silly with inane borough banter and whether readers would be interested in spies, statues, greyhound stadiums and Tony Blair's drinking hole.

There are of course books on Wandsworth that describe the rich and diverse history in more detail: from the arrival of the Huguenots to how each area expanded as dwellings evolved. But this miscellany sets out to give you a picture of the faces and places that make Wandsworth what it is.

Each London borough has its own specific landmarks. Wandsworth has Battersea Power Station, the busy Clapham Junction, Young's pubs and its former brewery.

But there is so much more hidden and ready to tell. How about the importance played by the landscape and geography? Take the River Wandle. This river was once one of the most famous fishing rivers in Britain, and Admiral Nelson gathered his thoughts here when back from battle. It was also home to a multitude of working mills which gave Wandsworth recognition throughout Europe for the many industries it catered for: textiles, leather, paper, calico and flour to name but a few.

Imagine the bustle of this eleven mile stretch of water through to the 1900s before the mills died out and the Wandle became abandoned. Pollution nearly killed the river a few years ago, but through regeneration programmes, it is beginning to thrive once more.

Gathering facts for the book has also given new perspective to certain areas. The view of Battersea's St Mary's Church right on the banks of the Thames at low tide, with modern glass apartments gleaming adjacently, is one of the borough's best views. The lover's lane steps leading down to Wandsworth Road. The Gothic building off Trinity Road, Peter Sellers on Balham, Daniel Defoe hiding out in Tooting. All are explained in *The Companion*.

Hopefully this book will give you nuggets of local history that you never knew existed. There are even some facts that have been left aside, so if you think there are stories out there worth knowing about, then keep Wandsworth's eclectism alive by getting in touch.

The Wandsworth Companion website is kept up to date, so please have a look round for more Wandsworth miscellany!

Rod Gilmour
July 2009
www.wandsworthcompanion.com

The Wandsworth Companion

The greatest autograph hunter

The Companion can lay claim to the borough once having the world's greatest collection of letters from the rich and famous. For years they lay unearthed before a great grandson of the original collector, who died in 1855, brought them to light and they went on view in Devon in 1930. John Ward, of Clapham Lodge, Clapham Common was the owner of thirty-nine embossed volumes containing 5,000 unpublished letters from celebrities right across the globe. These weren't just any old letters. The great musicians, poets, soldiers, diplomats, authors, royalty and politicians of the day were all featured, recording the crucial events at that given time.

The volumes included: Lady Hamilton's last letter to Nelson; Sir Walter Scott's letter before he left England for Rome on his last trip; Sir Christopher Wren complaining over building worries at Hampton Court Palace; Guy – the founder of Guy's Hospital – writing of his dealings in the South Sea Bubble shares; Danton and Robespierre on the French Revolution; early Presidents of the United States and private letters from George IV's wife on dealing with divorce. All lay untouched in a Clapham house for decades.

Five murals

'Oasis', Thessaly Road by Brian Barnes. A history of the world's flora and fauna.

'Tapestry of Life', Elspeth Road, SW11 by Christine Thomas, 1983. Celebrating ecology and depicting Adam and Eve.

'The Bathers', Thessaly Road by Brian Barnes. Wandsworth locals photographed at the seaside and depicted on the mural, it's about ordinary people.

'The Puzzle', Plough Road, SW11 by Christine Thomas, 1981.

'Battersea in perspective', corner of Dagnall Road and Culvert Street, SW11. Another Barnes epic. Painted in 1988, it depicts an aerial perspective, while it also reveals how many celebrated aviators came from the area.

Brian Barnes has been painting murals around London for around thirty-five years. His depictions of Wandsworth life are classic Barnes: large-scale, colourful and designed in collaboration with local groups. He was educated at the Royal College of Art between 1966-1969 and has been based in Battersea since 1967. His most famous mural was 'The Good, the Bad and the Ugly' on Battersea Bridge Road, which was a protest against new buildings. The 276ft mural was demolished in 1979. Others include the 'Violette Szabo' mural in Stockwell, 2001. It commemorates the locals who gave their life in the war and was listed in *Time Out* as one of London's top ten murals. However,

'Tapestry of Life', Elspeth Road, SW11 by Christine Thomas, 1983.

controversy surrounded the mural in 2005, when Barnes added a painting of Jean Charles de Menezes, and this new section was removed soon after.

Dulka Road, Clapham, SW11

In 2000, No. 10 Dulka Road went on sale. The familiar sounding name of one of Indian cricket's most popular figures, Sachin Tendulkar, meant the house received huge interest from sub-continent parties and ex-pats living in London. The owner at the time, Tom Gueterbock, had his change of address cards adorned with an image of Tendulkar, while it became a running joke for his friends to say they were 'going round Sachin's for dinner.'

An Earlsfield inventor

According to *Industries of Wandsworth* (1898), Mr R.G. Lacey of Earlsfield is the inventor of 'very valuable apparatus for saving life at sea'. He patented 'The Improved Drift Buoy and Line Apparatus' which helped stranded vessels communicate with shore. The publication says: 'It is a life buoy so fitted when thrown into the water, a sail is automatically raised, by means of which the buoy can be blown inshore taking a strong line with it'.

A quote on Clapham Railway staff in 1879

'The staff of railway employees are respectful and obliging to passengers; there is none of that bull-dog growl in reply to questions which characterize some men with surly dispositions who fill public positions.'

War in Wandsworth:
the beginning of the Blitz 1940

2 September: The first bomb fell which made way for a new bunker on the sixteenth fairway of the Roehampton Golf Course.

7 September: The main attack started at 5 p.m. with 300 bombers and seventy-five escorted fighter planes. Two hours later followed another wave of 250 bombers. Battersea was hit numerous times thanks to its network of railways, power stations and gas works.

8 September: Putney receives first attacks as bombs land on its Lawn Tennis Club and police station in Upper Richmond Road.

Du Cane Court in Balham

A Second World War urban legend surrounds this lovely art deco building, which is believed to be the biggest private apartment block in Europe. It is thought that Hitler wanted the building to be a German headquarters for himself and Wehrmacht and Waffen SS officers if the German invasion was successfully achieved. The fact that Du Cane Court is supposed to resemble a Swastika from the air is yet to be confirmed, as is the flight route with bombers told to turn left at Du Cane Court and head back home to Germany.

Bombs, casualties and rockets
– the effects of war

Number of bombs:	2,100
Incendaries, Oil bombs, AA Shells:	40,000
V-1s or flying bombs:	124
V-2s or rockets:	7
Domestic property in 1939:	76,000
Destroyed:	4,157
Damaged:	14,575
Lesser damage:	53,969
Civilian casualties killed:	1,301
Seriously injured:	2,191
Slightly injured:	4,205
Population in 1939:	340,000
Population in 1945:	251,510

Two war tales

A German bomber pilot who bailed out of his plane landed on a roof in the Clapham Park area in September 1940. He soon appeared at the top of the stairs where local residents were sheltering in the basement. Apparently he kept repeating: 'Police! Police! London!', the only English words he knew.

Wandsworth High Street was damaged later that year when the Old Bull public house was hit next to the Wandle. According to one humourous spectator close to the scene, 'it was a pity it wasn't the old town hall… they want a new building and that bomb might have done a bit of good, but then, Jerry don't oblige like that!'

Battersea on the big screen

The Royal Park has knocked the London Eye off top spot as the most popular filming location in London. Here are some films over the last ten years to have been filmed in Wandsworth: *102 Dalmatians, End of the Affair, Snatch, Wilde, Imagine Me &You, V for Vendetta* and *Stormbreaker.*

Wandsworth has also seen a resurgence in the number of requests for filming in the borough. Here is a list of known requests over the last few years:

03/04 – 547
04/05 – 610
05/06 – 670
06/07 – 807
07/08 – 960

The landlady's man

In 1954, Borough Councillor Clem Gethin published *I Denounce the Rent Tribunals* as a result of dissatisfaction and injustice experienced by landladies. Since the book, he appeared at tribunals all over London as he won back justice for 'landladies (and other leasers of furnished rooms) in that all disputes between landlady and tenant shall be tried at a properly constituted Court of Law according to the traditional and hallowed English legal rules of justice'.

Some blue plaques in Wandsworth

Gus Elen, music hall comedian, Thurleigh Avenue.
Jack Hobbs, cricketer, Englewood Road.
G.A. Henty, author, Lavender Gardens.
Edward Thomas, essayist, Shelgate Road.
Natsume Soseki, Japenese novelist, The Chase.

Wandsworth's most notorious gig

When The Stranglers came to the borough on 16 September 1978, it was soon to go down as one of Battersea Park's less serene moments. Rock historians will call it differently. Music lovers who were there will testify to that. Despite the band's growing stature, finding a venue was proving hard thanks to the Greater London Authority's stance on issuing licenses in the late Seventies. The Stranglers found a way past this by promoting their own show in the park at the end of a hot summer. The rest is history. After Spizz Oil, the Skids and Peter Gabriel had warmed the crowd up, The Stranglers then whipped them into a frenzy with a succession of hits before hired strippers came on during 'Nice N' Sleazy' and paraded round the stage. Most of the tracks were recorded for the band's classic Live (X-Cert) album, while images from the gig were revealed in most of the music industry's press. An ironic moment after most of the music media had rubber-stamped the band as sexists.

Minutes from Tooting Bec Court Rolls – XLIX 4 April 1421

A Court of Dom John Romeneye, Prior of Mertone, held there with view of frankpledge in the reign of King Henry V. Richard Hayward complains against Walter Castell in a plea of trespass. And he complains that Walter Castell's pigs have broken a building within the manors and destroys the peas and vetches there, amounting to 6s 8d.

La Wandsworth

At the beginning of the eighteenth century, it is believed that around 20 per cent of Wandsworth's 3,500 population were French. The Huguenots, French Protestants whose crest also forms part of the Borough's own crest, had descended on Wandsworth around 100 years previously after they fled France to avoid persecution. These protestant refugees tended to settle in areas where they could best make use of their skills; Wandsworth was attractive thanks to its industrial history and the mills located long the River Wandle. The development of the parish can be traced back to 1573 when Huguenot settlements sprang up in the area. During the seventeenth century, hat manufacturing by Protestant refugees was Wandsworth's most important industry. They had come from Caudebec in Normandy – the epicentre of felt and beaver hat-making. The composition of the liquid which was used to preserve the hare and rabbit skins was a secret only known to them. But during the Huguenot's sojourn to the borough, the secret was lost to France and the wealthy had to purchase their hats from refugees residing in England. The Huguenot's chapel is situated where the

Memorial Hall in Chapel Yard stands, off Wandsworth High Street. Its burial ground still survives off East Hill and was used between 1687 and 1849.

Mayor of Garratt – A right proper election

Not to be outdone by general elections in Parliament across the river, Wandsworth had its own boisterous elections from the middle of the eighteenth century. The first recorded Mayor of Garratt elections were held in 1747 and attracted up to 100,000 people. Like the more modern day Screaming Lord Sutch, candidates were drawn from the area's low-life (usually with a drink problem) with requirements for a quick wit and ability to entertain large crowds. Local pseudonyms included: Lord Twankum; Squire Blow-Me-Down; Lord Wedge; Beau Silvester; Sir Christopher Dashem; Sir George Comefirst; Sir William Airey; Sir William Bellows and Sir Jeffrey Dunstan, who was perhaps the most famous of all. Processions travelled down Wandsworth High Street and Garratt Lane before finishing at the Leather Bottle pub where the elections took place.

Dunstan was a second-hand wig seller from the West End who took his name from St Dunstans parish, where he was discovered on the step of the churchwarden's house in 1759. He was believed to have a disproportionately large head and was 4ft tall – all the requirements for the Mayor of Garratt. Dunstan's lively banter made him popular with the Garratt crowd, who twice returned him to office while he also became a close friend of John Wilkes, the radical MP. Dunstan's successor was Henry Dinsdale, who remodelled himself as Sir Harry Dimsdale. He was described as 'a deformed dwarf, little better than an idiot, who used to sell muffins in the streets about St Anne's Soho'. Like many of the previous candidates, he lived in a small attic near Seven Covent Garden, and in 1804 stood as the Emperor Anti-Napoleon, addressing his subjects as the 'Emperor of Garratt'. The tradition ended in 1826 although this was revived in 1992, when Sir Garibaldi defeated Thomas Rot in an election at the pub.

Four duels in Wandsworth

1652 Putney Heath: Lord Chandois v. Mr Compton. Mr Compton killed.
1810 Putney Heath: Mr Poynder v. Captain Smith. Smith Wounded.
1824 Marquess of Londonderry v. Mr Battier. No one hurt.
1798 Putney Heath: William Pitt the Younger v. George Tierney. No one hurt.

Industries and companies in Wandsworth

Thanks to the bustling life around the River Wandle, Wandsworth had a plethora of industry through the nineteenth century. These included Rainproof Cloth Co., Pianoforte Factory, paper staining, The Royal Wandsworth Paper Mills, horse flesh, calico printing, candle making, boat building, bone mills, fur dyeing, gas works, hat making, malt-houses, paper-staining, quill pens, steam launches, shawl printing and rope making.

Old advertisements are still present in the borough. (Image courtesy of Jane's London)

What are those concrete mounds on Clapham Common?

The Royal Air Force's retaliation on Berlin after the bombings in London in 1940 left Hitler outraged, and he ordered the Luftwaffe to concentrate on central London. Anti-aircraft sites were set up which consisted of a battery of three or four heavy guns. Before they were fired, the position, range and height of the planes were calculated using radar. This data was fed into an early computer prototype called a 'Predictor'. The guns were then fired in a pattern as laid out by the 'Predictor'.

Three prominent residents

Thomas Hardy, author, 172 Trinity Road, Tooting. Three-year lease.
H.G. Wells, writer, 28 Haldon Road. Lived here from 1891–1893.
Clement Atlee, politician, born at Westcott, 18 Portinscale Road.

Wandsworth Greyhound Stadium

The stadium was located to the north of King George's Park on a site now occupied by the South Side Centre. It opened in 1933 and could hold around 20,000 spectators. Greyhound races were held every week up until its last race meet in June 1966. Boxing bouts were also staged at the stadium. Earlsfield's famous Amateur Boxing Club, formed in 1946, stands close to the former site on Garratt Lane.

Wandsworth's architecture.

More prominent residents

Mary Ann Evans, better known as George Eliot, author, lived at 31 Wimbledon Park Road, Southfields, from 1859. Her day was usually a relaxing one. 'Glorious breezy walks and wide horizons, well ventilated rooms and abundant water'. *The Mill on the Floss* was written here.

An unusual news story

A woman who slipped on bird droppings and broke her arm has won a £20,000 payout. Lois Matcham, 64, was on her way to visit a grieving relative when she fell on the wet pigeon poo under the railway bridge at Clapham Junction station. She was unable to work and, after a four-year battle, Network Rail and Wandsworth Council have each paid her £10,000 in compensation. Ms Matcham said: 'I was walking with my cousin and we had gone single file under the bridge to avoid the droppings. But it was a wet day and I slipped. I landed in the stuff and could immediately tell I'd broken my arm.' She added: 'I'd just retired from Wandsworth housing department and was looking forward to working on some sculpture – something I couldn't do with my arm broken.'

The Battersea Bridge starlings

Clear, crisp, cold days bring the best out of this spectacular display. Battersea Bridge has the best known sighting, although the starlings seem to travel up the Latchmere Road to the church at the top of Clapham Common. The displays seem to get better every year (or is it because there are thousands more starlings?). In 2007, Starlings in Flight, a group of physicists, biologists and economists, revealed why they cause such a dramatic sight. Each individual focuses its attention on seven of its neighbours. And as the flock turns in the sky, it responds to the movements of these particular individuals. It doesn't matter how far these birds are driven apart, they will gradually move back towards each other. This goes against the popular belief that each starling simply watches out for the movements of the bird immediately in front of its companion.

The King's dinner to the poor, 1902

To celebrate the coronation of Edward VII, the King summoned the Lord Mayor to a meeting on 11 March where he wished that half a million of his poorer subjects in the Metropolis should be simultaneously entertained at dinner as His Majesty's guests at an expense to the King of £30,000. Events were held all over Wandsworth and the borough reported that these went off in relative peace.

A sporting mix

W.E 'Wilkie' Wilkinson
Along with Scotsman David Murray, Wilkie was one half of the most successful private sports car racing teams ever: Ecurie Ecosse. Murray was a gifted amateur driver who had a dream of creating a Scottish motor racing team in the Fifties. F1 was his objective but, in 1952, a team was organised around keen customers of Merchiston Motors, the Edinburgh business run by Murray and former Brooklands

MG tuner 'Wilkie'. It led to Le Mans triumphs in the late 1950s (a feat never to be repeated) although the original team continued until 1965 where it counted on the talents of Jim Clark and Jackie Stewart amongst its stable.

But what of the Wandsworth connection? Well, Wilkie had a pre-war business at his Bellevue Road Garage before the Second World War. With business slow, Wilkie met a Scottish crime reporter who formed part of a group who covered the Scotland Yard beat. They sat in their cars late at night writing their stories with an early deadline. As a consequence, their cars often broke down, and Wilkie made a nice little earner fixing the cars before heading back to his flat on Bellevue Road at 7 a.m. to start work all over again.

Frank Bruno – The Early Years

Britain's best-loved boxer started out as a nine-year-old at Wandsworth Boys' Club after watching Ali's comeback fight against Joe Frazier in 1970. The 'Fight of the Century' had given Bruno a reason to use his strength (or was it his mum who told him to do something useful?). His first experience was a painful one as the trainer had been tipped off as to Bruno's bullying manner. His son, Gary, was put into the ring and gave Bruno a lesson in unorthodox punching as his gloves 'thudded against my nose and my eyes watered like Niagara Falls'. He was later expelled from Swaffield Primary school when he was involved in a bout of fisty-cuffs on an excursion to the Houses of Parliament. He later came back as a guest of honour to present school prizes after his exploits in the ring.

Clapham Rovers

One of the earliest members of the Football Association, Clapham Rovers played on the Common in the 1870s but moved to Wandsworth Common in 1880. In 1879 they lost

1-0 to Old Etonians in the Cup Final before reaching the final the following year when they beat Oxford University 1-0. In front of a record 6,000 crowd at the Kennington Oval on 10 April, Clopton Lloyd-Jones scored the winner with an eightieth minute strike. Although they fielded a number of England internationals up until the turn of the century, Rovers dissolved as a club after the First World War. In May 2008, the winners' medal awarded to Rovers' forward Lloyd-Jones went up for auction where it outsold its estimate to fetch £4,200.

Jack Hobbs and the detective

One of England's finest cricketers, Hobbs lived first at 17 Englewood Road, where a blue plaque commemorates him, and later in Atkins Road, which has now been demolished. In his autobiography, Hobbs related to an incident on Clapham Common in 1906:

> A curious experience befell me on the outcome of a visit to Clapham Common, where I went to watch a friend play. Some team or other had failed to turn up, and the rival team asked my friend and his party to make up the match. I was invited to join and I hit up a century, knocking some balls into the pond. Then I started to bowl and had the ill luck to smash the finger of a detective, who was in the opposing team. I approached to apologise and, as we were standing around, he exclaimed: 'I've got you set; I know who you are.' His friends wondered what kind of criminal I might be, but he only told them my name at the end of the game, when they were delighted as if I had been Crippen!

The real meaning of 'Clapham'

From Captain Grose's *English Slang Dictionary*, 1796:

> *CLAP.* A venereal taint. He went out by Had'em and came
> round by Clapham home; (he went out a wenching, and got
> a clap). From C16 onwards. Now a vulgar, but until circa
> 1830 a polite, word for gonorrhoea. Early as a verb, even in
> such a figurative, anti-Puritan sense as 'Atropos clapt him, a
> pox on the drab' (1658).

The Leon Beron murder –
Brutal days in the borough

South London in 1910 was seen as a violent place.
With public outcries over crime aimed at the East End's
immigrant community, the media had a field day over the
Houndsditch murders and the Sidney Street siege. A murder
on Clapham Common on New Year's Day in 1911 brought
this new wave of crime to Wandsworth:

GRUESOME NEW YEAR'S MORNING DISCOVERY
– EAST END LANDLORD'S TRAGIC FATE

New Year's morning brought to light the perpetration,
under circumstances still shrouded in mystery, of a
gruesome murder on Clapham Common identified as
Leon Beron, aged forty-seven, a Russian Jew landlord, who
had been resident in the country upwards of fifteen years.
The discovery was made at 8 a.m. by a Cavendish Road
constable, while patrolling Bishop's Walk – an asphalted
pathway leading from the bandstand in a north-westerly

Clapham Common's bandstand.

direction towards Clapham Junction. Noticing something peculiar about the appearance of the furze bushes, he disclosed the dead body of a respectfully dressed man with his face covered with a coloured silk handkerchief. On this being removed, it was at once seen that the man's head had been severely battered, whilst two stabs had been inflicted.....
(*The Clapham Observer*)

The murder was known as the 'S' Case after the post-mortem. The letter 'S' had been roughly carved on Beron's cheeks. The black-and-red silk handkerchief, a paper bag from

Whitechapel, his legs neatly crossed and stab marks made by a strong, left-handed man were the clues that set the case up for policeman Frederick Wensley. Having failed to catch Jack the Ripper, Wensley set up making a name for himself in solving some classic murders as he soon went from chief constable to detective. He was known for being courteous to crooks, while he was never known to arrest a criminal while sat at a meal. He ultimately caught Beron's killer – Steinie Morrison, a Ukrainian refugee living in the East End. The jury took thirty-five minutes to find Morrison guilty of murder and he was sentenced to life. He repeatedly appealed to be put to death and, on 24 January 1921, weakened by a series of hunger strikes, he died in Parkhurst Prison.

The Falcon

Once touted as the longest bar in Britain. Have you enjoyed an ale in this classic pub? Here's what an old travel guide to Battersea had to say about this Clapham institution: 'It perpetrates the memory of a notable old Battersea hostelry of that name which stood at the corner of the lane leading from the Wandsworth Road to old Battersea Bridge. The landlord was one Robert Death, "a man whose figure is said to have ill-comported with his name, seeing that it displayed the highest appearance of jollity and good condition." There is a story to the effect that a merry-hearted artist named John Nixon, passing this house one day, found an undertaker's company regaling themselves at "Death's door". Having just discharged their duty to a rich nabob in a neighbouring churchyard, they had found an opportunity for refreshing exhausted nature. The artist sketched them on the spot.'

Ballooning in the borough

The sight of hot air balloons filling the SW skies was an all
too common sight at the turn of twentieth century. Notable
ascents included the first official flight from Putney, when
an aerial reportage on the University Boat Race was
conceived. In March 1893, the *Daily Graphic* commissioned
a 21,000 cubic ft balloon where it ascended by the Half
Moon pub. However, pipes soon had to be extinguished for
fear of explosion and the launch was delayed as 'would-be
helpers, some of them none-too-sober, were left hanging
on to the baskets' in a vain attempt to stop it. The balloon
was eventually cut free and went in a northerly direction
before landing miles away in Pinner.

Wandsworth also had a notable ballooning celebrity
through Leslie Bucknall. In his balloon 'Vivienne IV', he
broke the long-distance record which had stood since the
feat of the Great Nassau Balloon of 1836, when he made
an attempt from Wandsworth Gasworks to Vevey, near
Lake Geneva in November 1906. He covered an amazing
400 miles.

A summary of deaths during 1887

Measles:	147
Scarlet Fever:	60
Typhus Fever:	1
Diphtheria:	43
Whooping Cough:	153
Diarrhoea & Cholera:	245
Enteric Fever:	29
Small Pox:	0

'Three for a pound!'

The long-established Northcote Road market has recently seen local retailers priced out as rents have escalated. An action group has been set up to rightfully keep independent and local trade alive. Shopkeepers' anger has long since lingered in the borough and stretches back to the 1890s. During this time there were costermongers in Falcon Road, Northcote Road, St John's Road and Lavender Hill, much to the annoyance of other shopkeepers. The Ratepayers' and Tradesmen's Association lobbied for their removal on a number of occasions and in 1910 the costers were evicted from St John's Road. It meant Northcote became established as the primary local street market in the area.

Northcote's underground stream

The Falcon Brook's source was in Tooting and ran north-west to the Junction via Northcote Road. The name most probably derived from the Lords of Battersea Manor in the seventeenth century, the St Johns, whose crest was a rising falcon. Robert Death's Falcon pub was neatly positioned on the banks of the brook, too. As the years progressed, low-lit street lamps were positioned close to the stream as passers-by were prone to fall in from the banks. In 2007, Northcote Road and the surrounding areas found itself at the centre of mass flooding as the underground river system burst on to Wandsworth's streets. Schools were closed, buses were stuck and general havoc ensued.

Britain's first black Mayor

On 10 November 1913, John Archer was elected fourteenth Mayor of Wandsworth when he defeated the deputy leader of Municipal Reform, who was also a West End tailor. It is fair to say that Archer's victory was not without its controversy – mostly set up by Fleet Street. Up until Archer's nomination for mayor in the same year, there had been no reference to Archer's colour or origins. However, the news of his adoption and the fact that the Reform group was going to oppose him again led to national interest and journalists venturing to Wandsworth to pick up on the story. They came up with a series of lavish stories, including one that saw Archer originating from far flung outposts such as Burma. *Punch*, the satirical paper, was fascinated by the whole affair and saw the 'coloured gentleman... better than the present monotonous arrangement by which all our mayors are of the same hue'. Local politicians in Battersea were quick to react and stressed Archer's twenty-three years residing in the borough while highlighting how he closed his business every Wednesday afternoon so he could attend Board of Guardian Affairs. When he was elected , he said for the local classes: 'the greatest thing it has done is to show that that it has no racial prejudice and that it recognises a man for the work he has done'. Deeply popular, he died suddenly in July 1932.

Robinson Crusoe's Tooting

Before he wrote his classic island novel, Daniel Defoe was known as a luckless author who found trouble with the authorities from writing salacious pamphlets around

London. Born in 1661, he went bankrupt aged twenty-four before he took up writing. In 1701, he published *The true born and Englishman* and the following year *The shortest way with the Dissenters*. Soon afterwards he left the capital after the government issued a prosecution threat. A now-amusing ad was taken out in the *London Gazette*:

> Whereas Daniel Defoe, alias De Fooe, is charged with writing a scandalous and seditious pamphlet. He is a middle-sized spare man, about 40, of a brown complexion, and dark brown coloured hair, but wears a wig, a hooked nose, a sharp chin, grey eyes and a large mole near his mouth. Whoever will discover the said Defoe to one of His Majesty's principal Secretaries of State shall have the reward of £50.

Defoe was hiding in Tooting at the time but was discovered and stood in the pillory before the Royal Exchange. Fifteen years later, at the age of fifty-eight, *Robinson Crusoe* was published. Defoe's memory in SW17 was preserved in 1872 when a memorial was erected by the Defoe Memorial Manse in Charlmont Road.

From right rabble to royal park

Putney, Roehampton, Wimbledon and Battersea for centuries lay as marsh and bog lands. In the 1840s, Battersea fields had a sour reputation, mainly thanks to the infamous Red House tavern, which eventually closed in 1852. This was the first step in turning the fields into a Battersea park. Parish meetings were held to demean those who frequented the fields, where in the hotter months gipsies pitched their camps and gambling, immorality and prizefighting took place. In 1843, Thomas Cubitt suggested to the Parliamentary Commissioners of the Woods a royal park, and this request was eventually realised when the park was opened on 28 March 1858. But what of Battersea Fields? This was a place renowned for scurrilous and scandalous activity. In a report from the *London City Mission Magazine*, a Thomas Kirk wrote:

> ...and surely if ever there was a place out of hell which surpassed Sodom and Gomorrah in ungodliness and abomination this was it. Here was the worst men and the vilest of the human race seemed to try and out vie each other in wicked deeds. I have gone to this sad spot on the afternoon of the Lord's day, when there have been from 60 to 120 horses and donkeys racing each other, foot-racing, walking matches, flying boats, comic actors, shameless dances, gamblers of every description, conjurors and drinking booths. It would take a more graphic pen than mine to describe the mingled shouts and noises and the unmentionable doings of this pandemonium. I once asked the pierman how many had landed here on a Sunday. He told me that according to the weather up to 15,000, but up to 40,000 would have come from the various land roads.

Ye ol' late-night kebab

Located at Farmer Hall in Battersea, the Old House at Home was a tiny thatched hut where beer was sold direct from the cask and could only be drunk on premises. It was also famous for the 'egg flip'. This consisted of newly-laid eggs taken from the hens nest, beaten up in hot ale or porter, sweetened with sugar and sold to persons who 'preferred roaming around at midnight or in the small hours of the morning'. Texas Fried Chicken eat your heart out.

Oyez, oyez, oyez

Wandsworth Common resident Peter Moore has the ultimate voice and is London's world-renowned town crier, a tradition dating back to the Battle of Hastings. In 2008, at the age of seventy, he celebrated thirty years in the job and is believed to be the only full-time crier. His job has taken him to India, the United States of America, Russia, the Philippines, Hong Kong, Japan, Taiwan, Australia and New Zealand. His motto, 'Have bell will travel' has also seen him leading a parade, opening a school fete or welcoming visitors to London. He is also used for promotional purposes, whether it is at a tourist attraction or opening a pub. As the Mayor of London's official town crier, he can be seen around London at various locations such as Tower Hill, Trafalgar Square, Parliament Square or Piccadilly Circus, spreading the word of London to tourists. He always starts with 'Oyez, oyez, oyez' and ends with 'God Save the Queen'.

Ghosts I

Landlord Felwyn Williams and his wife had only been at the Plough Inn on Clapham Common a matter of weeks in 1970 when they discovered strange scenarios occurring at night. The top floors of the pub had long been reputed to be haunted and it wasn't long before they saw the presence of a woman in her thirties, staring into space with long black hair. Within weeks, Mr Williams had left the pub saying that he had an acute awareness of Sarah, while describing the experience akin to a mild electric shock lasting up to a minute. Rex, the landlord's dog, refused to venture upstairs while the ghost publicity left the pub in a bad state of affairs as far as the tills were concerned.

The Comic's Common

Thomas Hood (1799-1845), perhaps best known as a writer of comic poems, went to school at the Clapham Academy in the early part of the nineteenth century. He penned *Ode on a Distant Prospect of Clapham Academy* a few years later, where extracts reveal his experiences as being none too memorable:

Ah me! Those old familiar bounds!
That classic house, those classic grounds,
My pensive thought recalls!
What tender urchins now confine,
What little captives now repine
Within yon irksome walls!
There I was birch'd! There I was bred!
There like a little Adam fed
From Learning's woeful tree!
The weary tasks I used to con!
The hopeless leaves I wept upon!
Most fruitless leaves to me!
The summon'd class! The awful bow!
I wonder who is master now,
And wholesale anguish sheds!
How many ushers now employs,
How many maids to see the boys
Have nothing in their heads!

The Poet's Common

Shelley, the celebrated English poet, also had his misgivings for Clapham, although he did find love here. In 1810, Shelley passed on from Eton to University College, Oxford but his college career barely lasted six months and he was summarily expelled for his opinions in the *The necessity of Atheism* pamphlet. But, unlike Daniel Defoe, he was free to roam the streets and set up lodgings in central London. At that time, his sisters were boarders at Mrs Fenning's School on Clapham Common and he paid frequent visits there. However, on one visit he found one of his sisters wearing an iron collar – an instrument of torture which Mrs Fenning made her pupils wear as a cure for 'poking'. After getting over this hurdle, Shelley soon found himself entwined with another boarder, sixteen year old Harriet Westbrook. He wrote to a friend, 'She has thrown herself upon my protection. I declare, quite ludicrous, yet, how flattering a distinction.'

All the Eights

Britain has a host of eclectic annual awards, from Fish Shop of the Year to Public Loo of the Year. The National Bingo Caller of the Year has been going for a while, but unfortunately, no Wandsworth caller has ever reached the finals. 2007 saw the borough's best efforts, however. Jason Owen reached the Southern Regional final but was just pipped at the post by Melanie Ceazar, from Enfield. The Wandsworth club has also played host to the National Final in 2002. That year the celebrity host was Lesley Joseph, from the much-loved television series, *Birds of a Feather*. Lesley lives near the club and every now and then dabbles in a game. She told the enthusiastic audience that she will often sneak into the club just before 'eyes down' and settle herself down near the back with a set of six books to try her luck.

Duel of honour… and hilarity

Battersea Fields and Putney Heath have been well documented as being the most popular places to settle a dispute over the years, but perhaps the most high-profile of these was between the Duke of Wellington, who vanquished Napoleon's troops at Waterloo in 1815, and the Earl of Winchelsea in 1829 at Battersea. The slight absurdity of the event left many to predict that duelling was on its last legs, as noted in the *Morning Herald*'s account on 23 March:

> The city was thrown into ferment this morning by a report which seemed so utterly improbable that at first few believed it. We were among the incredulous, thinking it a story fit only to amuse male and female old ladies – those gossipers in and out of petticoats. But every third person we met told us seriously how His Grace the Duke of Wellington had taken offence at his lordship's, the Earl of Winchelsea's, letter about the King's College; how the aforesaid noble Duke had challenged the Earl; how the said belligerents had agreed to meet, stand up, and fire at one another at the distance of 12 paces, like sage statesmen and true Christians; how they accordingly did meet this morning in Battersea Fields among the cabbages; how his Grace, the Prime Minister of England, shot at his lordship… how, thereupon, the noble Earl fired his pistol in the air; how the Earl's second presented a written apology and so the affair was amicably settled.

Yes, it was true. The Duke of Wellington, the first warrior of his day, the conqueror of Napoleon, the Prime Minister and the author of a law which he says is necessary for the welfare of the Empire, placed himself in a situation where he might have been charged with murder…merely because a noble lord wrote a pettish letter, which even his best friends laughed at. No wonder the multitude break laws when the law-makers themselves, the great, the powerful, and the famous, set them at open defiance.

The noble lords wished each other good-morning and returned to town. About fifteen gardeners and labouring men, who were on the spot during the transaction, advised the noble combatants to settle the matter in dispute with their fists.

Tooting's Granada Cinema

Perhaps one of the finest cinemas in London, it once housed 3,000,000 people each year in its heyday in the Forties. Granada commissioned Fyodor Kommisarzhevsky, a Russian architect, theatre producer and one-time husband of Dame Peggy Ashcroft, to create the interiors. Built in 1931, it was considered his best work. A sweeping staircase with Gothic attributes led to a mirrored hall with arched mirrors, which in turn led to the swinging door of the grand circle. Usherettes, in gold silk blouses, blue trousers and pill box hats, blue cloaks and white gloved hands would take you to your seat under the massive brass candelabras that hang from a vast dark gold Gothic coffered ceiling that spans the whole auditorium. The auditorium held over 2,400 people three times a day, seven days a week before a lack of interest saw the cinema close in the Seventies. The

Tooting's iconic former cinema.

threat of demolition enabled the hall to gain its crown, that of a Grade I listing in 1999 and it is now a bingo hall.

At arm's length

Most football fans know their club's logo. But what about Wandsworth's? Following the merger with Battersea and the loss of Clapham and Streatham to Lambeth, new arms were granted in 1965 after the original chequers were granted in 1901. It features checks from the arms of the de Warenne Earls of Surrey, denoting that the area was part of Surrey until 1889. The teardrops represent the Huguenot exiles who came to the borough in 1685. The crest also has a dragon ship taken from the old Wandsworth arms, with four oars and four shields for the four parishes of the borough – Battersea, Putney, Tooting and Wandsworth. A sense of smell is also granted thanks to the sprig of lavender, signifying Lavender Hill. The dove is charged on the wing with four gold stars, one for each parish. The black dragon is derived from the dragon-ship in the crest.

Wandle magic

The old

Overlooked for over fifty years, neglected by new builds and frequented by fly-tippers, *The Companion* has spent many evenings trying to persuade people to believe the fact that the Wandle, one of London's lost rivers, was once Britain's most prolific chalk stream.

It was once revered by trout fishermen and the proof lies with Frederick Halford, one of the most famous of fly-fishers, who caught his first trout on a dry fly on the Wandle in 1869. The Wandle, regarded as London's second river, runs through an eleven-mile-long green corridor across four boroughs – Wandsworth, Merton, Sutton and Croydon – flowing north from Croydon and Carshalton to join the Thames at Wandsworth.

And before Halford came Admiral Nelson. When Nelson gave his love, Emma Hamilton, the funds to buy Merton Place in September 1801, it is believed that the river was even redesigned so that the Admiral could walk down to the end of his vast garden to fish the banks. Although naval duties saw Nelson battle bigger waters, he would spend as much time as possible back on the Wandle when time allowed. Despite having lost his casting arm in battle, he even taught himself to fish with his other hand. With one of the world's finest chalk streams just a short walk from his back door, he just wasn't going to be denied! Reports several years later even indicated a massive opening day haul in 1899 when a local resident took sixty fish from a 100 yard stretch in Carshalton.

With around ninety mills along the eleven mile stretch during Victorian times, the Wandle was one of the hardest working rivers in the world, producing everything from gunpowder to silk. As the borough became more influential, so the demand increased. However, the pollution from industry soon began to take hold on the Wandle. From one of the cleanest rivers, by the 1960s the river was effectively declared an open sewer.

The new

From its delta to its two sources, in Waddon Ponds in Croydon and its secondary source in Carshalton Ponds, the river's signposted heritage trail today provides almost uninterrupted cycling or walking along its banks, through more than a dozen parks and nature reserves.

Forget the surrounding tower blocks, cast your mind back to the green spaces of early Victorian times and it is easy to forget that much of the Wandle is surrounded by mass-populated areas. The trail is also complemented by a massive effort to regenerate the Wandle back to its former glory.

However, that dream was nearly scuppered two years ago when Thames Water made a horrendous mistake at its sewage works in Beddington and sent a cleaning agent into the river. It wiped out thousands of fish and twenty years of restoration in a single day. For what it was worth, Thames Water soon owned up and pledged £500,000 to help regeneration.

Volunteers and those close to projects on the Wandle stuck together and just a few years on there is burgeoning activity on the riverbanks.

River Wandle.

One of the successes has been 'Trout in the Classroom' – the Wandle Trust's award-winning core educational project since 2001. Every December the project visits participating schools to install specially modified aquaria, which are then seeded with trout eggs. Each trout tank aims to reproduce the natural conditions of river life for the little fish with the fish's survival rate bein 10 per cent higher in the classroom than in the wild.

From January to March, the kids watch the eggs hatch until they're ready to be released into the local river at the end of March. Teachers agree that elements of 'Trout in the Classroom' link seamlessly into almost all areas of the National Curriculum.

Wandle clean-up days are now a massive operation. At given dates throughout the year you will see volunteers comb different areas of the river to remove rubbish left by people who really have little clue as to the importance of river life.

Come the summer months and the riverbanks have recently come alive with annual events such as the Wandle Valley Festival, which is held each June.

The reality… for now

Extracted from *Somewhere Else* by Charles Rangeley-Wilson:

Earlsfield station exits on to a busy street right underneath the railway line. The dank air is ripe with the smell of pigeons. To the north a garage, then the road curves out of sight. I checked my map, crossed the road and turned north, then west past a motorbike repair shop and just beyond stopped at a small concrete bridge. Below, the water was clear enough for me to see dark stones and old tyres on the stream bed. From this bridge I could only see a few yards, so I walked back to the main road and headed south to find the Wandle Trail, a footpath which runs up the whole river. Right opposite the station there was a tackle shop, and I went in to ask whether there were any trout in the Wandle. The shopkeeper looked at me, not as if I'd asked a mad question, more as if he'd waited a long time for someone to ask it.

'They're in there,' said the shopkeeper.

The man my side of the counter agreed.

'Not many, I don't think, and no one fishes for them. You're not going to fish for them, are you?'

I admitted that I had this idea about catching a wild trout in London. He asked why, and I was embarrassed to give a reason. I don't know, I said to him, the world seems so f***ed, I just think a wild trout in London would mean that it wasn't. He nodded, and I relaxed and carried on. 'Used to be loads you know. They had a Royal Warrant on this river it was so full of trout and salmon.'

'I'm sure you're right.'

'My mate had one last year,' added the customer. 'Mostly when they do get caught, they're taken home for breakfast. Up the road the river splits in two, and there's a deep bit by the steel pilings. Try a worm along there.'

I thanked them, and as I left they both wished me luck.

I found the spot easily, a spit of land with a path worn through with nettles, a shallow weir upstream which shelved down to spill foaming water into a dark pool under the trees, where the air was cold. Downstream, the two streams met, bright green weed was anchored to rubbish and its flowers swayed in the current, while a few yards away Clapham trains clattered over a bridge. There were dace on the sill of the weir, some rising to small midges buzzing over the water surface. I walked upriver all day, from Earlsfield to Carshalton, through parks, and behind factories. I saw a fix. I couldn't find any trout.

Putney Lawn Tennis Club miscellany

1917 – Insurance cover was taken out against potential aircraft damage to the club's pavilion.

1923 – Club rule proved popular measure when whisky was reduced to ninepence.

1926 – An extraordinary general meeting was held to elect the first of two lady committee members.

1931 – Club funds were to be invested in a building society, on the proviso that the committee were satisfied that the money was 'easily withdrawable'.

Wandle Trail, one of the borough's hidden secrets.

Bombs dropped I

Putney, 1940:
9 Keswick Road
55, 57, 59, 61 West Hill
26 Lebanon Gardens
11 Valonia Gardens

Wandsworth, 1940:
Bank of River Wandle at Mapleton Road
13 Kimber Road
Junction of Twilley St and Kimber Road
Veritas Works, Garratt Lane

In search of suburbia in 1939

From a *Daily Sketch* columnist:

I am finding suburbia even more puzzling. Alighting from a 19 bus at Clapham Junction I found I wasn't even in Clapham. I was in Battersea (rates 13s 2d in the £, which seems high for such a poor quarter). On the journey down I remember that someone once told me that Clapham housed more red nosed comedians than any other suburb. In fact it has always been prime favourite with the theatrical profession from the days of Dan Leno to Gertrude Lawrence and Noel Coward, who were born there. So I expected a good laugh and looked forward to my arrival.

…As I walked the common in the drizzling rain, avoiding the ARP trenches, I looked at the fine old Georgian houses that flanked me at either side and thought of the prosperous merchants of London who once built these noble homes and settled there, driving each day from these country estates along the turnpike road to London to conduct their business. Converted into flats these homes may now be, but their dignity remains. Perhaps a little paint is needed here or there, but time cannot obliterate the beauty of that early craftsmanship.

...I have taken a great fancy to Clapham. They tell me the air on the common is finer than the South Coast and splendid for rheumatism. It covers a surprisingly small area (1,120 acres) and its population is only 60,000. But the common takes up a lot of room. While having no theatres, Clapham does have plenty of cinemas, which are all open on Sundays. It is interesting to compare each suburb in this respect. But I should not have thought Clapham with such a religious background, would allow Sunday entertainment at all.

...There is little fake about Clapham. It is solid and the view of the North Side as you walk the common will satisfy the most jaundiced eye. I'm going to take that walk again some day for sheer enjoyment. As I caught my bus home, I thought of the one contact Clapham still has with the old days that were – the two sisters in the stationer's high shop at 174. To have met them is to have known the glories that were once Clapham. Yet like all people who have something to swank about – Clapham doesn't.

Clapham at the movies

Picture houses were a popular pastime at the beginning of the twentieth century. The Shakespeare Theatre on Lavender Hill, which opened in 1896, was first devoted to drama until

1912, when it changed hands and was converted into a cinema 'with pictures interspersed with songs by high-class ballad and concert vocalists'. The period from 1908 until the beginning of the Second World War saw the rise and decline of cinema. The first of these, and probably the most popular, was opened in Northcote Road. Known as 'Bio-Picture Land' it changed to 'The Globe' in 1917.

Clapham's Roman stone

A great stone of considerable interest to the British Museum was found in 1912 at the Cavendish house estate on the common. The estate bears the name from the home of the eccentric chemist, Henry Cavendish, whose famous experiment to determine the earth's density made in his Clapham garden earned him the title 'the man who weighed the earth'. The museum said it was of equal importance to the 'London' stone – the original *millarium* from which all roads out of London were measured. The Clapham stone is thought to have been a first-century Roman altar stone.

The weeping nun

Clanking chains, uncanny noises and ghostly nuns have all been reported at 46 South Side, Clapham Common. Brooke House was a commercial college in the Thirties and a secret passage in the garden was believed to have formed part of an old nunnery. It ran under Clapham Park Ground near St Mary's Church. The legend goes that a grey figure is seen weeping near the passage and an old well. She had a baby which she dropped down the well and so overcome with remorse, she was ordained to return after her death and mourn for it.

Turpin's strip

The famous Dick Turpin is supposed to have made the Plough on St John's Hill his headquarters while he plundered all around him, including his favourite stretch, Garratt Lane. In 1735, two gentleman were attacked on the Upper Richmond Road by two highwaymen, one of whom was believed to be Turpin. The travellers were forced to dismount and give up their purses. On another occasion, some Guildford waggoners were attacked by footpads near Putney Heath.

Miller of Wandsworth

English Civil War struck in 1642 and although Wandsworth was seen as loyal to the King over Parliament, it didn't end well for our local miller according to legend, as the thousands marching against the King were soon dispersed by Cromwell's soldiers and the miller was executed:

Hark to the clamour of fife and drum,

Three thousand Surrey men marching come.

Their van by snow white banner is led,

And the Miller of Wandsworth he walks at their head.

A humble petition they come to present,

At the doors of the Houses of Parliament.

And windows fly open to catch up the strain,

King Charles! King Charles! Shall be brought home again.

Rafael Sabatini

Walk past the houses on Albert Bridge Road, look across to Battersea Park and the carriage drive and play out a typical scene from Victorian Wandsworth. Lovers in hand, horse-driven carriages and the peace of the park. 81 Albert Bridge Road also housed a very famous author of the times. Sabatini's most famous works have been translated into the classic swashbuckling films *The Sea Hawk*, *Scaramouche*, and *Captain Blood*, but he produced thirty-one novels, eight short novel/short story collections, six non-fiction books, numerous uncollected short stories, and a play.

Born Jesi, Central Italy, 1875. Son of Maestro Vincenzo Sabatini and Anna Trafford. Recreation: fishing. Died 1950, Switzerland.

A great storm victim

Huge crowds from all over London came to witness the aftermath of the Great Storm in 1780. Wandsworth seemed to be worst affected. One pamphlet, written by a Roehampton resident, suggested that 130 large trees were uprooted within a distance of a mile, while one 40ft tree was seen to have been carried over 130 yards. On 11 June there was a burial in Putney of one of the storm's victims. William Bovan was thirty-six and a blanket maker by trade. His height was recorded as 3ft and was described as being 'of weak intellect and much given to drink. His head was abnormally large in proportion to the rest of his body, his voice was harsh and his condition generally unhealthy.'

Harveys' shenanigans

Marco Pierre White's cooking on the Bellevue Road caused a stir in the food world. Celebs, critics and cuisine lovers from all over the world came to Wandsworth Common in the late Eighties when MPW won his Michelin stars at Harveys. There were some classic stories too. Kitchen tantrums, passionate rendezvous', throwing out diners and general cooking pressure mayhem ensued. Here is one extract that *The Companion* wishes it had witnessed:

I was at reception one evening with my nose in the bookings. I heard a voice and said, 'I'll be with you in a minute, sir. Can you hang on?' 'Are you going to insult me?' came the reply. I looked up and there, in front of me, was a mountain of a man. He was about 6ft 7in, had been in for dinner and was clearly drunk. 'Look, if I decide to insult you I'll choose my time and place to do it.' He went back to his table and an hour later they left and took a right up St James's Drive. It was about midnight and I decided now was the time so I got two chefs to fill two buckets of water and sent them off. I was having an espresso later when Man Mountain reappeared, perfectly dry but clutching two carrier bags full of soaked clothes. 'You threw a bucket of water over me,' he said. 'I didn't,' I replied. 'I know nothing about this. Did you try chasing the people who did this?' And his response was, 'Have you ever tried running in a wet suit?' Great line that.

Wandsworth Olympians:
past, present and future

The Past

Wandsworth's greatest Olympian was born on 24 March 1889. Albert Hill lived in Tooting and went on to become a gold medallist in the 800m and 1500m at the 1920 Olympics. Deprived by the First World War, Hill was written off before the Antwerp Games after being beaten by a South African at the AAA Championships. At thirty-one, he was deemed too old for both events but he won a reprieve after winning his case against the AAA after being dropped. Determined to bring back success, Hill set off by boat and after a dodgy crossing and inadequate accommodation, he ended up arriving at the stadium by lorry. The Belgian organisers had further scuppered Hill's chances when they put all the star runners in one heat in order 'to give the also-rans a chance'. Coached by Sam Mussabini, Hill, however, won a double in two days that was not replicated by a British middle-distance runner until Kelly Holmes did it in 2004. After a life in south London, he moved to Canada shortly before the Second World War, where he died in 1969.

The Present

Along with Nicole Cooke, Emma Pooley kick-started Team GB's medal rush at the 2008 Beijing Olympics. Riding the race of her life in the Women's Time Trial, she collected GB's first cycling medal (silver) of the Beijing Games, in the shadow of the Great Wall of China. The Wandsworth girl only took up competitive racing three years prior to Beijing. A Cambridge University engineering graduate, Pooley rode to success on a bike specifically designed for her 5ft 2in frame. Born in 1982, she currently resides in

Switzerland where she works as a soil engineer, while her achievements in China will never be forgotten.

The Future

Darius Knight is the rising star of table tennis. Born in 1990, he is a serious hope for London 2012. Knight calls table tennis his saviour after learning the trade in a battered shed in Battersea, saved from a life of crime and drugs. He was spotted in 2002 when Knight and three friends would often travel after school to hone their talents in a rundown garden shed. From an essentially broken family on a fourth-floor council flat estate in Wandsworth, Knight was subsequently sent up to Sheffield where he plays full-time at the national academy. He is a former national under-21 champion and represents Great Britain on the World Pro Tour. Knight is a shining hope and an example of how sports stars can be plucked from the most unlikely of places.

A film quote… from Love Actually

Prime Minister:'I'd like to go to Wandsworth, the dodgy end.'
PM's chauffeur, Terry:'Very good, sir.'
[They drive to Wandsworth]
PM's chauffeur, Terry:'Harris Street. What number, sir?'
Prime Minister:'Oh, God, it's the longest street in the world and I have absolutely no idea.'

From pitch to Parliament

Wandsworth's finest cricketer, Jack Hobbs, was also once seen as the perfect candidate to stand for Parliament.

After he had scored his 126th century, equalling W.G. Grace's record in 1904, his friends felt that to seat him in Westminster would be merely a fitting tribute to such a great achievement. Arrangements were made for Hobbs to run as a Liberal candidate from one of the Wandsworth divisions. But Hobbs had last-minute thoughts and went off the idea and decided to concentrate on his runs and not running for Parliament.

Balham – Gateway to the South

If you haven't heard Peter Sellers' classic 1958 sketch, then search for it on *The Companion* website. The sketch saw Sellers talk you through the sights and sounds of Balham using old footage in a mickey-taking American travelogue style. The pronunciation of Balham remains a comedy classic:

> …We enter Bal Ham through the verdant grasslands of Battersea Park, and at once we are aware that here is a land of happy, contented people who go about their daily tasks in truly democratic spirit.
>
> …This is busy High Street, focal point of the town's activities. Note the quaint old stores, whose frontages are covered with hand-painted inscriptions, every one a rare example of native Bal Ham art. Let us read some of them as our camera travels past.
>
> 'Cooking apples! Choice eaters!'
>
> 'A song to remember at the Tantamount Cinema!'
>
> 'A suit to remember at Montague Moss!'
>
> 'Cremations conducted with decorum and taste.'

This shows the manifold activities of Bal Ham's thriving community – but in quiet corners, we still find examples of the exquisite workmanship that Bal Ham craftsmen have made world-famous: tooth brush holesmanship.

Now let us see a little more of the town. Here is the great park, covering nearly half an acre. This is where the children traditionally meet by the limpid waters of the old drinking fountain, a drinking fountain that has for countless years, across the vast aeons of time, give untold pleasure to man, woman and child. Beside this fountain, donated by Able Councillor Quills as long ago as 1928, the little ones sit around a trim nursemaid and listen spellbound and enchanted as she reads them a story,

'With one bound, he was by her side. Nora felt his hot breath on her cheek as he ripped the thin silk from—'

We are now entering Old Bal Ham. Time has passed by this remote corner; so shall we. But Bal Ham is not neglecting the cultural side. This is Eugene Quills, whose weekly recitals are attended by a vast concord of people. He has never had a lesson in his life. Such is the enthusiasm of Bal Ham's music lovers that they are subscribing to a fund to send Eugene to Italy. Or Vienna. Or anywhere...

Night falls on Bal Ham. From Quill's Folly, Bal Ham's famous beauty spot, which stands nearly 10ft above sea level, the town is spread below us in a fairyland of glittering lights, changing all the time: green...amber...red...red and amber...and back to green. The night life is awakening!

The Al Morocco Tea Rooms...
'Hey, miss?'

'Yes? What d'you want?'

'Pilchards.'

'They're off, dear.'

'Oh. Baked beans?'

'Off.'

'Oh. Meat – meat loaf salad?'

'That's off, too.'

'Pot of tea?'

'No tea, dear.'

'Well, just milk then.'

'Milk's off.'

'Roll and butter, then?'

'No butter, dear.'

'Well, just a roll!'

'Only bread, love.'

'I might have just as well have stayed at home!'

'Oh, I dunno, does you good to have a fling occasionally!'

And so the long night draws on. The last stragglers make their way home and the lights go out one by one as dawn approaches and the bell of Saint Quills' Parish Church tolls ten o'clock. Bal Ham sleeps. And so we say farewell to this historic borough, with many pleasant memories – and the words of C. Quills Smith, Bal Ham's own bard, burning in our ears...

Broad-bosomed, bold, becalmed, benign,

Lies Bal Ham, four-square on the Northern Line.

Matched by no marvel save in Eastern scene,

A rose-red city, half as Golders Green,

By country churchyard, ferny fen and mere,

What Quills mute inglorious lies buried here?

Oh stands the church clock at ten to three?

And is there honey still for tea?

'Honey's off, dear.'

The original lovers' lane

In the 1930s there was a pathway in Clapham that seemed to weave a magic spell for a long and happy marriage. Six houses used to lie twenty-nine steps up from Matrimony Place, off the Wandsworth Road, near the parish of St Pauls, Rectory Grove in SW4. (It's close to the train station and the passage going up is barely 5ft wide). The residents of the six houses used to tell of courting couples who 'made their trysts in the Place', while they made sure they were never disturbed. They believed that the Place brought luck to lovers while even the local vicar saw the twenty-nine steps as a sign of happiness for scores of married couples. It seemed like Clapham's own aphrodisiac and, not surprisingly, owners had handsome offers turned down for the six properties. As one resident put it back then, 'Like our neighbours, we should never dream of quarrelling. If we should be nearly forgetting ourselves we have only to say to each other, "Now, now! Don't forget this is Matrimony Place" – and it is all over in a moment.'

La Clapham

A touch of France came to the borough in the eighteenth century in the form of Voltaire, the revered author. He must have made an impression for Voltaire Street in SW4 is named after him. After Voltaire had pushed his way into the French Courts system, he was addressed by a rival, Chevalier, as a parvenu. Voltaire used his creativity to write some damning epigrams which in turn led to a savage beating and being thrown into the Bastille. After a short imprisonment, he was liberated on the condition that he

Matrimony Place.

set sail for England. He landed in May 1726 and lived with Viscount Bolingbroke for a short while before returning to France in 1729. Four years later, Voltaire's *Letters concerning the English nation* were documented, where the Frenchman highlighted the capital's impressive attitude towards religious tolerance.

The ghost of Tooting churchyard

The theory goes that this ghost sits on top of a grave overrun with weeds with the tombstone inscripted, 'Gone, but not forgotten: never shall thy memory fade!' Word has it that it must be the ghost of Mrs Thumber, who lived in the area in the 1830s. Some said she was a busy-body who liked nothing better than go into other people's houses and learn about their business all day long. However, she was believed to be an honest church worker, was popular in the village and was instrumental in the building of the new church before her death.

The joke's on Wigan

Thanks to music hall comedians at the beginning of the last century, the very mention of Tooting, Aberdeen and Wigan put audiences into hysterics. The 1920s, however, put Tooting into a different light. The locals were serious about where they lived and it was up to 'The Grand Old Man of Tooting', the Reverend Bevill Allen, to be its PR saviour. 'There is no justification for the numerous jokes on Tooting. It is a very serious place and the people have improved enormously in the last twenty years.' It sparked the following verses in the *Streatham News*:

Oh! Tooting is a serious place
(Hush! Cease your silly hooting!)
There is no reason for the fun
That people poke at Tooting.

'The people have improved,' declares
The Grand Old Man of Tooting
'Enormously, and now the place
is on a different footing.'

Will humorists please therefore try
When jokes they are recruiting
To stick to places father North
And not to touch on Tooting?

Meanwhile, we might perhaps find out
By history up-rooting
Who claims to be the very first
To put the 'toot' in Tooting?

Derby days

The Epsom Derby used to propel thousands of locals on to
Wandsworth's streets. The build-up would start early when
hundreds would make the trip to Surrey by foot on the eve
of the big race, stopping in the many drinking holes. After
the race, the stakes were raised and locals had to be on their
guard, such was the frivolity of the returning race-goers. As
one Balham resident put it, 'We had a regular fair outside the
Duke of Devonshire on Derby night in the Thirties. There
was a horse trough there in those days, full of water, and I've
seen more than one policeman go into it over the years.'

Twenty20 and all that

Although the first recorded cricket match in England had taken place around three years earlier, a series of matches were announced in April 1700 on Clapham Common, the first such reported matches in London at any rate. The periodical *The Post Boy* stated that the matches would consist of ten gentleman per side, while they would be played on the Common with prizes of £10 a head per game 'and £20 the odd one'. This implies that the matches were single innings only and were all to be played in one day. 300 years on and the shorter Twenty20 game is thriving, but could this be the first ever?

Night-time Charlie

In 1830, an Act of Parliament ended the duties of the watchbox, heralding the start of Night Police being employed in the borough. Previously, watchmen had patrolled a particular beat; their duty was to go twice round during the night. They were usually aged men, hired on small salaries, while they were provided with a great coat, lantern, a pole, rattle and their watchbox. In Clapham Common and the surrounding areas there were twenty-five watchmen's boxes, which were colloquially known as 'Charlie's'.

Blair in Wandsworth

As the Seventies ended, former Prime Minister Tony Blair was just starting out in his legal career when he moved into a small house in the Tonsleys. 41 Bramford Road was owned by Charles Falconer, later to be prefixed by Lord and one of the original 'Tony's Cronies'. It was shared by four in total, according to the 1980 Electoral Roll. Both Falconer and Blair were also activists in the same local Labour Party. They shared a passion for rock music and, with the arrival of the Eighties, both men were clearly keen to keep the spirit alive. Whether they wiled their spare hours away in the Alma Tavern is another question, but what is known is that Falconer was able to memorise the B-sides of practically every hit single of the Sixties.

Olympians II

Claude Percy Buckenham, Association Football. Born 16 January 1876, Wandsworth. Won gold, 1900.

Charles Darley Miller, Polo. Born 23 October 1868, Putney. Won gold, 1908.

George Arthur Miller, Polo. Born 6 December 1867, Roehampton. Won gold, 1908. Brother to Charles.

Gordon Lindsay Thomas, Rowing. Born 27 March 1884. Won gold, 1908 (Coxless Pairs). Won silver, 1908 (Coxless Fours).

The first railway

Forget George Stephenson. Wandsworth was where the railway made its introduction and where the first iron railway in England was authorised by Parliament. On 21 May 1801, a bill was passed as an 'act for making and maintaining a railway from the town of Wandsworth to the town of Croydon, with a collateral branch into the parish of

Carshalton.' The owners called it the Surrey Iron Railway Company. There were no railway engines as such in those days; the power was supplied by horses, which pulled the wagons over the rails. Nothing like it had ever been seen before. The new railway could pull twelve wagons loaded with stones and carrying fifty men, weighing a total of fifty tonnes. That was with one horse. The effort was immense and far removed from the effort by modern train bosses to get Britain's rail network in working order.

Another first

While on the subject, do you know where the origin for the word 'tram' comes from? The Surrey Iron Railway was constructed by Messrs Jessop & Outram. From the latter's name we have the modern word 'tram'. Think of Wandsworth the next time you're in Manchester or Eastern Europe.

Rare, indigenous plants in the borough

Rumex Sanguineus – Blood veined dock. Found on the bank of a ditch on Lavender Hill, between nursery and footpath.
Pulcher – Fiddle Dock. Found by the footpath of Battersea Bridge to Lavender Hill.
R. Hydrolapathum – Great Water Dock. Found in wide ditches. Battersea Park.
Mentha pulegium – Pennyroyal. Prefers damp conditions, close to the River Wandle.

The Boat Race

The race may start in Putney and row away from
Wandsworth, but that doesn't stop *The Companion*.
Professional watermen were used at first to direct the
crews. In 1877, 'Honest John Phelps', around aged seventy,
judged the result of the two crews. It was a tight race
that year and there were no finishing posts. According to
one hostile observer, Phelps shouted out: 'Dead heat to
Oxford by five heat'. It was the last time that professional
watermen were involved.

Ghosts II

Mark down 30 January, wait until dark and venture out
on Putney Heath at midnight. It is rumoured that the
headless ghost of Charles I can still be seen as he gallops on
horse towards London. It is believed that he rode the old
Portsmouth Road on this date to see his children at Ham
House before his execution in 1649.

Battersea Dogs' Home

Set up in 1860, Battersea Dogs' Home has become a national
institution, housing around 700 dogs and cats. In 2000, poet
Steve Tasane took up a residency at the Dogs' Home to
record a series of poems. The following is one example:

The Dogs of Battersea Dogs' Home

Here's a soccer player about to score,
Here's Oliver Twist asking for more,
Here's your uncle after a night on the booze,
And Screaming Jay Hawkins howling the blues.

Here's a beached seal, stuck on a rock,
And a death row con, watching the clock,
Here's Granddad snoozing on a Sunday afternoon,
And Billy the Kid in the Last Chance Saloon.

Here's a front-line soldier with a butterfly tummy,
Here's my baby, coming to mummy,
Here's a big fat Sumo, panting for breath,
And a gentle giant licking children to death.

Here's a kid in detention who's still giving cheek,
And a babe on a catwalk whose gait is unique,
Here's a raging bull who's trashing the place,
And a princess in exile maintaining her grace.

Here's Caesar the Lurcher who wants to have fun,
And Grobble the Greyhound who refuses to run,
Here's Tyson the Pit Bull who's looking for love,
And Herman the Corgie who thinks he's the Guv.
Terry the Terrier is trembling in terror,
Toying with a Toyota was a terrible error,
Who's laughing? Leonardo the Labrador, that's who,
'cos Sidney the Shih-tzu is teaching Shiatzu.

A crafty King Charles must be running a number,
He's King of the Cha-cha-cha, Salsa and Rumba,

Runs rings round the kennel hands, hoards every treat,
If not creating chaos he isn't complete.

There's a Siberian Husky who gets rather frisky,
Changing his blanket is reportedly risky,
Although he's been snipped he is sadly misled,
Wants a litter of puppies to pull in his sled.

There's DJs and MCs and manic street preachers,
Compulsive scratch-scratchers and horrible screechers,
Occasional canines who constantly cower,
Plus a litter of Spice Girls with puppy dog power.

There's brown-nosers, ball boys and even librarians,
There's one vegetarian and two Rastafarians,
There's hairy ones, scary ones and perfect gents,
A collective bark and a million scents.

Borough bridges

A list of dates when the bridges in Wandsworth were erected:
1729 – Putney Bridge
1771 – Battersea Bridge
1873 – Wandsworth Bridge
1873 – Albert Bridge

The greatest rowing race?

Ernst Barry (England) v. Richard Arnst (New Zealand),
August 1912.

Starlings over Albert Bridge.

Thousands of people lined the Thames by Putney to witness the 'champion of the world' race, an honour that an Englishman had failed to win for thirty-six years previously. By 1.30 p.m. on the day of the race, crowded launches were afloat, while hawkers were selling colours of each skuller. Arnst had won the toss and selected Surrey station, while the boats were held at the start by 'Bluff' Cordery and 'Dogett' Cobb. Just after Hammersmith Bridge, Barry nudged ahead and he soon passed Barnes Bridge in 19 minutes 23 seconds, 13 seconds ahead of Arnst. Wild celebrations could be heard back at the Vesta Rowing Club in Putney when news filtered through and when he returned to the club, he was handed the Sporting Life trophy and a cheque for £1,000.

Borough birds

Peregrine falcon (Falco peregrinus)
The bird of prey is colonising the capital as part of its national recovery and there are around 2,000 pairs in the UK. More commonly a cliff-nesting species, peregrine falcons also take to nesting on large buildings in cities. Battersea Power Station is home to a breeding pair who have raised young every year since the turn of the millenium. The inner Thames marshes are an important feeding area for visiting peregrines in winter.

Mount Nod

Cedars Road in Clapham was the cause of much hysteria in the Thirties following a cryptic passage in a government report on historical monuments in London. In the back gardens of several houses on the street, stood a 20ft mound. Excavations took place, archaeologists were called for opinion, the press believed that Clapham's history could now date back to Stonehenge times. The mystery was heightened and the following possible theories were outlined:

– It could be prehistoric, possibly serving as a shrine to the Celtic water-god, Nuud, who was worshipped from the mound's summit.

– Possibly a Roman burial barrow from the second century AD.

– It could be a pile of rubbish excavated in Charles II's time when a nearby house was built.

– The mounds are in a straight line at right angles to the Thames, and may have marked paths down from the Clapham heights to a safe crossing from Battersea marshes.

The White Square

Hidden between Clapham Park Road and Clapham High Street, White Square was once a peaceful hamlet surrounded by lush green fields. The red brick cottages and the village inn are said to have housed Admiral Nelson; Nelson's Row and Nelson's Grove perhaps indicate as much. Legend also suggests that Dick Turpin is connected with the Square. Turpin is said to have taken refuge in a house in the neighbourhood and hid his booty down a well before fleeing. The well is thought to be in existence beneath the floor of one of the cottages.

The Grid

Southfields is now seen as an affluent area – close to 100 years after the Grid plan had finished being constructed. The development was seen as an outstanding success, while developers had done their job in enticing families with the ideal of homes that were spacious and attractively designed. The designs can still be seen today, with leaded-glass front doors and attractive tiles in many families' front doors. Each street seemed to have their own intricacies in design at a time when the Arts and Crafts movement held great appeal. One such property held a great example of this era when a Mr Merredew, of Engadine Street, left his mark on the movement with some outstanding design on his house in the top left-hand block of the street. He commissioned a design of 'fine, tall windows, cast-iron trim over the porches and elaborately moulded pediments in the gables of the roofs.' With the arrival of the 1920s also came the improvement of public transport. Southfields was one of the areas in south London to benefit as the No. 39 bus route ferried passengers from Wandsworth Town Centre to Southfield Station. However, with the buses coming through the Grid, it obviously got too much for one resident after years of peace following the Second World War. 'Are we to wait till the houses fall down round our ears – they shake fearfully,' he told the *Wandsworth Borough News*.

Hammer blow

With built-up areas comes the inevitable decline of birds in the capital. The yellowhammer is one such bird, as W.H. Hudson noted in 1898 in *Birds of London*. He was damning on the residents of Wandsworth, too, writing in his findings that the borough 'are hardly deserving of such a bird'. The yellowhammer is in decline but can now be seen in country lanes. Hudson gives us another guilty verdict. 'He does not know that there are places on the earth where the furze-bushes are unblackened by smoke, where at intervals of a few minutes the earth is not shaken by trains rush thundering and shrieking, as if demented, into and out of Clapham Junction'. For posterity, the male has a mustard-coloured head, streaked with feathers of dark brown.

Queen gets feet wet

The bridge over the Wandle by the old Arndale Centre is so inundated now with traffic and daily activity, it is little wonder that life rarely revolves around the famous river below. Not so back in the early seventeenth century. The bridge's origins are lost in the mists of time, but legend has it that Elizabeth I was even involved with the bridge's history. In 1601, she was trying to cross the bridge when she found it in a very bad state of repair. The Queen was forced to ford the river herself before issuing a repair order, which was completed the following year.

The name game

The ten most popular names in the borough from 2006:

Boys	*Girls*
1. Jack	1. Olivia
2. Thomas	2. Grace
3. Joshua	3. Jessica
4. Oliver	4. Ruby
5. Harry	5. Emily
6. James	6. Sophie
7. William	7. Chloe
8. Samuel	8. Lucy
9. Daniel	9. Lily
10. Charlie	10. Ellie

Wandsworth Tattler

Prisoners at the famous jail were rarely informed of goings-on in the vicinity during the Thirties. So with typical prison humour, an unofficial magazine was published in 1939 entitled *The Tattler*. Produced by an inmate, the magazine was put together by cotton thread and was hand-written. Editorial was light on the ground, while it contained various remarks on staff and fellow inmates. Spoof ads read 'Have you tried the new scientific method of bathing? If not, visit 'Oppy 'Arper, our famous dry bath specialist and banish soap and water forever.' A correspondence section also made it in. 'To Disgusted, Wandsworth. We have investigated your complaint about "The Creeping Screw" and have ascertained that it is Officer Coles. He uses special rubber soles for the purpose.'

The brown dog affair

In a quiet spot near the English Garden in Battersea Park stands a statue of a small brown terrier, although the story behind the statue belies the spot where it now stands. In 1906 in Latchmere Recreation Ground, stood a drinking fountain memorial (for people and dogs) that was erected:

In memory of the brown terrier dog done to death in the laboratories of University College in February 1903, after having endured vivisection extending over more than two months and having been handed over from one vivisector to another till death came to his release. Also in memory of the 232 dogs vivisected at the same place during the year 1902. Men and women of England, how long shall these things be?

The early part of last century were experimental times in medicine research, and there was a large pro-vivisectionist lobby who took exception to the statue and it was soon under twenty-four hour police guard. In 1907, University College students attacked the statue with a crowbar and sledgehammer. Interrupted by police, the attack was unsuccessful but a few weeks later, students from London, Oxford and Cambridge led a demo march on the statue and another to Trafalgar Square. Battersea residents, who had respected what the statue stood for, responded with vigour and the 'Brown Dog Riots' ensued. It took a year for calm to be restored, but the council were concerned about the possibility of more riots and the statue was finally removed in 1910. A week later, 3,000 demonstrated in Trafalgar Square. In December 1985, a new brown dog memorial was erected by Geraldine James, a Battersea resident and anti-vivisectionist, on the present site.

An interesting inmate

George McMahon made his entry into prison in 1936. On 16 July that year he had tried to shoot Edward VIII, who was returning from a military ceremony. He was sentenced to twelve months hard labour for his botched attempt. A few months later the prison had a visit from Edward's brother, the Duke of Kent, who was amused when prisoners in the workshop rose to bow to him.

A prison note

Capital punishment was rife in the Thirties, as was Mrs Violet Van der Elst, who went on a fervent crusade against the death penalty – and no more vociferously than at Wandsworth. The irrepressible lady had inherited a lucrative shaving cream business from her Belgian husband, headed up three corporations and was a director of twelve. Any imminent hanging led Van der Elst to the prison where she used to ram her car against the front gate of the Governor's quarters.

So imagine the following case as described by *Time* magazine in 1935:

Leonard Albert Brigstock, one time petty officer in His Majesty's Navy, had been sentenced to hang for slitting the throat of Chief Petty Officer Deggan on the gunnery training ship *Marshal Soult*. Crusader Van der Elst assembled 65,000 signatures to a petition for a reprieve; offered to hire a brain surgeon to prove that Brigstock was insane. Nonetheless the trap was due to drop under Brigstock at 9 a.m. one day last week in south London's Wandsworth Prison. Shortly before 9 a.m. Mrs Van de Elst went sweeping up to the prison gate in a cream-coloured limousine, shouting through a loudspeaker, 'They are hanging an innocent man. We have last-minute evidence to prove it.' Three loudspeaker vans were already driving back & forth blaring out 'Abide With Me'. A mob of fifty sandwich men paraded with signs. Mrs Van der Elst's supreme inspiration, three airplanes zoomed above the prison, trailing banners, 'Stop the Death Sentence.' Promptly at nine o'clock, the trap dropped under murderer Brigstock. 'Gentlemen remove your hats,' cried Mrs Van der Elst, falling on her knees. Later she said: 'I pay £12,000 ($60,000) income tax and I have a right to be heard by the Government. I am going to protest against every execution in England from now on… The Government dare not arrest me.'

Four businesses no more

Alf Gover's Cricket School

Established in 1928 and run by the former Surrey and England fast bowler, the indoor school held a fascinating charm for those who were taught the game from within the walls on East Hill. Matting and netting were everywhere, nothing seemed new and the cricket shop was a veritable feast of the game's paraphernalia. Alf joined the school in 1938 – he was to retire from the game in 1947 – and was to continue throwing down balls to eager cricketers right into his eighties.

Price's Patent Candle Factory

The company was acknowledged as the world's leading manufacturer soon after it bought out a previous business in 1847. And the reason? Price's were well ahead in advanced science. Knowledgeable shareholders were quick to get the best price for the company. It boiled down to the distillation of schist, in France, followed by scientific discoveries on Boghead coal and Rangoon petroleum, leading to the discovery in America of vast sources of petroleum. In turn this produced its source of portable light.

Ram Brewery

The famous advertising hoarding 'We've been around the bend since 1831' still lights up a dreary Wandsworth one-way system. But the hops smells from the brewery have stopped. They've stopped for a few years now ever since Young & Co ended more than 400 years of heritage by shifting production of its ales to Bedfordshire. The company sold its historic Ram Brewery site for redevelopment which will see flats, retail and a micro-brewery as part of the 5½ acre site. Established in 1675, the brewery won countless awards and has been visited by the Queen over the years. And in an era when mergers and takeovers were commonplace, the survival of a family undertaking for well over a century was no mean achievement. Having always been in Wandsworth, Young & Co.'s Brewery was a family firm; a number of its employees could trace ancestors back several generations within the company. Thorn was one such family name. In the 1860s, Alexander, a collector for the brewery, was attacked by footpads on Putney Heath but still managed to save the considerable sum he was carrying with him. One hundred years later, his great-grandson, Kenneth, was working at the Ram.

Arding & Hobbs

Established in 1876, two energetic young men (namely Arding and Hobbs) were destined to build up the largest furniture and drapery store in south London. It had started with a small shop on Wandsworth High Street before the duo purchased five shops on the Falcon Road in 1881, five years after starting in business. In 1885 the buildings on the corner of St John's Road and Lavender Hill were erected before the pair moved in. The store became known as the 'Harrods of the South' and employed 400 staff. Although a fire in December 1909 virtually destroyed the building, it continue to trade until the chain went into administration in 2005 and was sold off to Debenhams.

A review of Young's Special London Ale

The Ram Brewery may have moved, but that doesn't mean to say that Young's beers have totally vanished from Wandsworth's armoury of pubs. Here are the tasting notes for the Special from renowned website 'Beer Pages':

Spread Eagle pub, Wandsworth.

A former CAMRA Champion bottle-conditioned beer, this is brewed with Maris Otter pale ale malt, 'phenomenal amounts' of Fuggles hops (according to Young's) and is late-hopped with Goldings too. It pours a striking amber colour, with a thick off-white head. The nose has a lovely grassy, herbal, almost minty quality with fine purity and depth. On the palate it is creamy and immediately chocolaty in both texture and dry, bitter darkness. There is fine plum fruit with a plum-skin bitterness, and that racy, endive and chicory hop quality adding crispness and definition.

Oldest tube

East Putney: opened 3 June 1889.
Clapham Common: opened 3 June 1900.
Clapham North: opened 13 September 1926.
Clapham South: opened 13 September 1926.
Tooting Broadway: opened 13 September 1926.
Tooting Bec: opened 13 September 1926 (named Trinity Road until 1950).
Balham: opened 6 December 1926.

The Borough's greatest…

The greatest dustman

Whenever a dustman in Wandsworth saw Ted Foster bounding down the street, they would say: 'Here comes Tiny.' 'Tiny' was the borough's VC hero – ex-corporal Edward Foster – born and bred in Tooting and Inspector of Dustmen for Wandsworth Council. He picked up his nickname in the trenches, an example of British Army irony with him being 6ft 1in and tipping the scales at twenty stone.

The greatest cartoonist

A blue plaque resides at No. 40 Nightingale Lane for revered cartoonist H.M. Bateman. He was born in Australia in 1887 and came over to England as a baby. He became well-known for his series of cartoons, the 'Man Who…' which depicted social gaffes and were published in many periodicals. His skill led to him becoming the highest-paid in his field.

Incidentally, blue plaques around London are a common sight. The scheme was first started in 1867 by the Royal Society of Arts and many of the plaques took on a chocolate brown colour. An example can be seen near Thomas's School in Broomwood Road marking William Wilberforce's house.

The greatest pub name

The Cat's Back on Point Pleasant. This pub is full of quirks from around the world and wouldn't look out of place in a props department. What's in the name? Well, it's unusually named after a landlord's cat that ran away and then returned. Simple as that.

The Bravo murder

This gruesome Balham murder is one of the great unsolved mysteries of the Victorian era. In 1876, Charles Bravo, a young barrister, was found poisoned at his mansion home, The Priory on Bedford Hill in Balham. There were so many suspects in the case that the finger of guilt could not be pointed at anyone; to say that the case resembled a game of Cluedo is an understatement.

Was it Florence, the unliked but beautiful and wealthy wife? Was it Mrs Cox, the housekeeper whom Bravo was going to sack to save money? Or even Dr James Gully, Florence's physician, twice her age and who had made her pregnant and subsequently performed her abortion? Throw George Griffiths, Florence's stableman, who had a grudge against Bravo and had a supply of the poison in the stables, into the mix and the mystery held centre stage in national newspapers that naturally thrived on the darker side of Victorian bourgeoisie.

It took Bravo, who was thirty-one, three days to die after the poison, potassium antimony, had been slipped into his bedside glass of water. On his death bed, detectives failed to entice Bravo into saying who had poisoned him – he remained calm before his death – and they took this to mean that he had wanted to commit suicide. Decades later it was discovered that antimony caused this reaction.

Detectives suspected Florence, who was depicted as petty, hard-drinking, selfish and dictorial. She had pursued an affair with Gully, physician to the Queen Charles Dickens and Benjamin Disraeli, and after one already unhappy marriage, she wed Bravo and left Gully extremely jealous. Bravo had married her for the money, while Florence was more interested in respectability and prosperity.

On the night of the murder a furious row developed between Florence, Mrs Cox and Bravo. The housekeeper's motive was twofold; she would have been left to fend for three sons if sacked by Bravo and wanted her boss out of the way to keep her job.

The murder is further heightened with one final twist. Dr Gully was believed by some to have been Jack the Ripper. Even Agatha Christie got in on the act but, after examining evidence in 1968, struggled to identify Gully as the likely culprit and declared the case how the rest of intrigued Londoners also saw it – a complete mystery.

The nearly meet

The Jules Rimet World Cup Trophy may have been sniffed out by Pickles the dog in a bush in Streatham, but it was nearly handed back at a midnight meet in Battersea Park in 1966. After being stolen from a stamp exhibition in Westminster Hall, Edward Bletchley, a former soldier, was accused of the golden theft and for the attempted blackmail of Joe Mears, former chairman of the Football Association and Chelsea Football Club. Mears had agreed a £15,000 ransom for the return of the World Cup, which was to be traded in the Royal Park. As the exchange grew nearer, Bletchley became suspicious of a transit van – a police back-up team – and fled the scene. He soon found himself in Brixton prison before finalising a deal with police to let a lady friend visit him in prison. Days later the World Cup was found by Pickles and a reward was given to its owner by the FA.

Doc Tooting

The name Dr Matthew Keith Hall doesn't ring a bell for you or me. But he is better known as Harry Roy Hill, the BAFTA award-winning English comedian, author and television presenter, who began his career with popular radio show Harry Hill's Fruit Corner. Born in Surrey, Hill was educated at Cranbrook School in Kent, and holds a medical degree from St George's Hospital in Tooting. He is St George's most famous doctor and surgeon on television.

So what about St George's history? Well, life for the hospital actually started out over the river in 1716 when Henry Hoare, William Wogan, Robert Witham and Patrick Cockburn (collectively a banker, religious writer, brewer and curate) decided to open the Westminster Public Infirmary in Petty France. By 1732, and after already moving to larger premises, the Governors were forced to move again. A new hospital was built at Lanesborough House on Hyde Park Corner, expanding to 250 patients within twelve years. By the 1930s it was apparent that the Hyde Park site was too small to cope with the needs of modern medicine and after the establishment of the NHS in 1948, Aneurin Bevan, its founder, announced that St George's would be rebuilt on the current Tooting site. The final move from the Hyde Park Corner site took place in 1980 and services have continued to expand throughout the 1990's up until the present day.

Wandle Womble

Wimbledon FC, the defunct club that played in south London and now plays under AFC Wimbledon, once used a Womble as a club mascot. It was named 'Wandle' after the river that ran close to Plough Lane. After a naming competition in which the final name was chosen by *The Wombles* author, Elisabeth Beresford, the club announced that the new Womble would be known as 'Haydon' after the railway station on the corner of Plough Lane. Beresford created the Wombles in 1968 and the characters became famous in the 1970s as a result of the BBC programme. Beresford was a freelance ghost writer and children's book author and married to BBC sports commentator husband Max Robertson.

Deep down

At the beginning of 1944, the Second World War air attacks began to take shape and on 13 June the V1 assault began, followed on 8 September by the V2 rockets. It was a common theme for Londoners until 27 March 1945. Thirty metres below Clapham North tube station lies a deep-level air raid shelter, which was one of eight built across London during the Second World War. The others were Clapham South, Common and North, Stockwell, Oval, Goodge Street, Camden Town, Belsize Park and Chancery Lane. Taking two years to build, it housed over 8,000 troops from 1942, in a plethora of parallel tunnels over two miles long. Transport for London rents a number of the chambers across the capital while the Clapham tunnels remain unused.

Locations:

– Clapham North – At rear of car park on Bedford Road near Clapham High Street. And on the west side of Clapham Road, opposite 383 Clapham Road.

– Clapham South – On Clapham Common at the junction of Clapham Common South Side, Nightingale Lane and The Avenue SW4. South entrance is on west side of Balham Hill opposite Gaskarth Road.

– Clapham Common – Behind hoardings on Clapham High Street at junction with Carpenters Place.

Perfect for wine storage, could we see a new fad in Londoners? Rent out a chamber, get a dinner party going and finish the night with The Jam's 'Going Underground'. In 1948 the Deep Tunnel at Clapham South also provided temporary accommodation for 236 Jamaican immigrants who had sailed to Britain on *The Windrush* while in the 1950s it became a youth hostel during the Festival of Britain.

Borough baggage

Where does your luggage go after Heathrow's Terminal 5 staff forget to put it on the right carousel? Answer: Tooting. The little-known secret occurs down the Broadway every week at Greasbys Auctioneers, the South London firm founded in 1919 by Henrietta Greasby. Bidders have the element of surprise as they don't know what they're bidding for in the suitcase, but the going rate for a case is anything up to around £50.

Gothic hangout

The Priory was built in the early nineteenth century in a style known as Strawberry Hill Gothic and first became a hospital in 1866. Name ring a bell? It does for the likes of Kate Moss, Paul Gascoigne and Ronnie Wood but little is known of the interior décor considering the exterior has been pictured in numerous tabloids. The Roehampton clinic is one of fifty-three specialist units treating patients (who are known as A, B, C etc) suffering from the following problems: depression; schizophrenia; degenerative and neurological problems; brain and spinal injuries and eating disorders.

What's that Gothic building off Trinity Road?

Imposing and exuberant, the Royal Patriotic Victoria Building has had a colourful history. It was originally erected as a home for orphaned girls of servicemen after the Crimean War. Today it stands as one of Wandsworth's famous landmarks, with an eccentric restaurant – Le Gothique – serving up acclaimed French fare. The building played its part during the First World War when casualties from the trenches were delivered there via a specially built railway, while emergency marquees within the Victoria's grounds held up to 1,800 casualties. During the following war, the Victoria was then MI5's special operations centre and housed suspected spies and other criminals, including war criminals like Rudolph Hess. The eccentricity of the place has even seen the building owned by Andy Taylor from Duran Duran.

Putney Velodrome

London once had an abundance of cycling tracks around the capital and Putney must have had one of the better tracks, as the velodrome held numerous world cycling and walking records. The first meeting was held on 8 August 1891 and the last on 11 August 1905. The track was situated in the area now between Hotham Road and Landford Road before it was bulldozed. Velodromes seemed to have a habit of coming to a sticky end. Across the river from Putney stood the Lillie Bridge cycle track off Lillee Road in Fulham, but was destroyed by a riot amongst spectators at an athletics meeting in 1887.

Bombs dropped II

Roehampton:
27, 28 and 30 Roehampton Gate, 11 September 1940.
Richmond Park Golf Course, 10th Fairway, 31 October 1944.
25 Roedean Crescent, 14 October 1940.

City tropics

The following transcript is an early description of Battersea Park's sub-tropical garden, which opened in August 1864:

It's enough to make you go and see for yourself, wherever you live. It is situated at the head of the ornamental water surrounded by sloping banks, parterres and rolling lawns. In this region flourish palms, fern trees, plants and large leaves, gigantic grasses and the climbers and creepers of Equatorial forests and jungles. India-rubber trees, castor oil plants, Japanese honey-suckle, Chinese privet, the banana of Abyssinia recalling the expedition of Magdala; the papyrus plant of Egypt, the veritable bulrush of the Nile, the beautiful scarlet foliage of the dragon's blood tree from South America, the large-leaved tobacco plant, the caladium esculentum from the Windies, the *neottopteris australis*, besides a variety of vegetables from the tropics. Eastward of the garden is situated the Peninsula, containing some of the choicest combinations of floral work, resembling in pattern the most exquisite tapestry. The Alpine point gives a miniature representation of the valleys and mountain-peaks of Alpine scenery.

Tooting Bec Lido

At ninety metres, the Lido is the largest freshwater pool in England and host to the World Winter Cold Water Championships. It opened on the eastern edge of Tooting Common in 1906. The pool has a seaside feel with the array of colours on the cubicle doors and the expanse of blue water. The Lido was nearly closed as a result of Wandsworth

Tooting Bec Lido.

Council's financial cutbacks in the 1990s, which in turn resulted in the closure of another lido at King George's Park. Tooting is also open on Christmas Day when swimmers can brace the chilly, but azure-like, waters with the Mayor and sing along to Carols at the same time.

Greener the better

Just over 20 per cent of the borough is covered by private gardens. Preliminary results from the council's garden survey show a thriving habitat for a diversity of animals. Over forty different types have been recorded: the robin, blackbird, frog, fox, tawny owl, green woodpecker, stag beetles and bats.

10 trains of thought...
Q&A with Clapham Junction

For those early birds, Clapham seems to be getting busier and busier. How many people use the station?
Pedestrian flow surveys were carried out during September 2006 for future building works and from this it was estimated that approximately 70,000 people use the station daily; 60 per cent who interchange and 40 per cent who start or finish at Clapham.

That's a lot of customers. There must be a lot of trains passing though then?
Yes, there are 1,600 South West trains and 1,900 Southern trains each day. This will increase with the East London Line orbital link in 2012.

How many staff work per day on average?
101 employees work across the station, with our station operating trains 364 days a year with twenty-four hour operation on some routes.

They must have come across some peculiar items over the years which have been left at the station.
Well, we have had one blow-up doll, which was eventually collected!

What are the most common items left?
Umbrellas, followed by mobile phones.

Do you have rules for train spotters?
Many of our train enthusiasts know the rules and regulations when on station property. We do keep a careful eye on some, as we have had people jump down onto track to get better glimpse of train numbers. Also we do not allow flash photography, as it may dazzle drivers.

Who is the current long-serving member at CJ?
We have a lady who started working at Clapham Junction in 1970 in the train depot off Plough Road.

What are the most memorable events at CJ?
Unfortunately it would be the Clapham rail disaster, but Clapham Junction also suffered significantly from bomb damage during the Second World War.

What are the five most commonly asked questions to staff?
Where is the way out?
Which is the platform for Gatwick?
Which is the platform for Waterloo?
Which is the platform for Victoria?
Do I need a ticket/Where do I get a ticket?

Which is the most popular platform?
That would be Platform 10 to London Waterloo.

Differing voices

The nineteenth-century Prime Minister Benjamin Disraeli, also a writer, created an Earl and Countess of Roehampton in his autobiographical novel *Endymion*. The poet Gerard Manley Hopkins studied at the Jesuit seminary at Manresa House. In sharp contrast, the risqué writer Frank Harris twice lived in Roehampton with his extremely young wife-to-be, Nellie O'Hara. Harris said that Roehampton and the French Riviera were his favourite places in the world. Yorkshire-born writer and journalist Arthur Ransome, the famed *Swallows and Amazons* author, was obliged to live with relatives in Balham in 1904. He called Balham 'the ugliest and most abominable of London's unpleasing suburbs' and soon decamped to Chelsea. Luckily for local estate agents, Balham's reputation has improved immeasurably since then.

Summerstown

Light industrial enclave located beside the River Wandle, where Tooting meets Wimbledon. The street named Summerstown links Plough Lane with Garratt Lane. From the late Middle Ages there were mills beside the river, which frequently flooded the area. 'Dutchmen' are recorded as manufacturing brass plates for kettles and frying pans around 1631 and there is also evidence of Huguenot silk weaving and wig making here. In the eighteenth and early nineteenth centuries, the hamlet provided labour for the Wandle's mills. The writer and poet Edward Thomas cycled through Summerstown just before the outbreak of the First World War and described the scene in his evocative travelogue *In Pursuit of Spring*:

The main part visible was twenty acres of damp meadow. On the left it was bounded by the irregular low buildings of a laundry, a file and tool factory, and a chamois-leather mill; on the right by the dirty backs of Summerstown. On the far side a neat, white, oldish house was retiring amid blossoming fruit trees under the guardianship of several elms, and the shadow of those two tall red chimneys of the electricity works... A mixture of the sordid and the delicate in the whole was unmistakable.

(Extract reproduced courtesy of *Hidden London*)

Summerstown's Romanesque parish church of St Mary was completed in 1920 and is now Grade II listed. Wimbledon, Lambeth and Streatham cemeteries are to the west, south and east respectively. There's greyhound racing at Wimbledon stadium. Summerstown has absorbed the former hamlet of Garratt, and is now itself being lost within Earlsfield. Contemporary housebuilders in the Garratt Green area claim that this is Earlsfield, despite the SW17 address.

Well I'll be hanged...

The tolling of the bell, the corridors of silence, the prisoner's weight taken, the trap door opening and the tightening of the rope. Wandsworth Prison was awash with hangings from its very first execution on 8 October 1878 when Thomas Smithers, the Battersea Murderer, achieved that accolade. A year later and Catherine Webster became the only woman to be hanged after being found guilty of murdering her boss. In 1949 John Haigh, the 'acid bath murderer' was executed after being convicted of dumping one victim in sulphuric acid to destroy evidence. About 1,000 protesters massed at the prison the morning of Derek Bentley's execution on 28 January 1953. Controversially, Bentley was executed for his part in the murder of police officer Sidney Miles. His accomplice, who actually shot Miles, was Christopher Craig. Craig was only sixteen – too young to be executed. In 1993 Bentley was pardoned for the sentence – forty years too late – and today the famous double-meaning in the 'let him have it Chris' is still controversial.

Her Majesty's inmates

In his inauguration speech, Barack Obama payed homage to slain civil rights' leaders as he vowed to revive the spirit of sacrifice during the global recession. But what is his link to the borough? A sour one in truth, and concerning Prisoner 059184 at Wandsworth Prison. Named as R.G.S. Sneyd, also known as James Earl Ray, the assassin of Martin Luther King. King died in 1968 when he was shot as he stood on a balcony of the Lorraine Motel in Memphis, Tennessee. James Earl Ray, who confessed to the murder during his trial, was arrested at Heathrow Airport in June 1968 after trying to use a forged passport and held in Wandsworth Prison, South London, while he awaited extradition to the United States. He initially admitted the murder but later retracted the confession and his insistence of his innocence has since been backed by Dr King's own family. But prosecutors said Ray fired the fatal shot from the bathroom of a nearby hotel, using a hunting rifle, and he was sentenced to ninety-nine years in prison. Records from Ray's time in Wandsworth, released in March 2001, showed US authorities feared he would be killed in prison. They also revealed Ray told prison guards he blamed black Muslim groups and Dr King's own supporters for the assassination.

Biggs escapes from the Borough

It was 1964, a year that saw the last hangings take place in Britain. The headline writers would be further compounded by the news that Ronnie Biggs was going down for thirty years at Wandsworth Prison for his part in the Great Train Robbery. Hailing from Lambeth, Biggs was a member of the fifteen-strong gang which attacked the Glasgow to London mail train at Ledburn in Buckinghamshire on 8 August 1963 before making off with £2.6million. After just over a year of sewing up postbags at Wandsworth – much to the prison warden's delight – Biggs had obviously had enough of life inside. On 8 July 1965, Biggs and fellow inmate Eric Flower were exercising in the yard at around 3 p.m. when a red removal van parked outside the prison walls close to the officers' houses. A trap door opened in the van's roof and a scaffold was raised. For any lone passer-by, it must have taken a moment to wipe the eyes before seeing a ladder being put over the wall and into the yard. Both men legged it towards the wall, along with two other prisoners looking to take their moment. Officers in the yard failed to catch the prisoners thanks to fellow inmates getting in the way and the group sped off up Trinity Road after transferring into a green Zephyr car. They turned onto Bellevue Road and Biggs began his ritual of sending back postcards to the UK to the police authorities. Biggs was on the run for more that thirty-five years, where he lived in Spain, Australia and Brazil, before returning to the UK of his own accord in 2001.

St Mary's Church, Battersea, home to Sir Edward Wynter's tomb.

Battersea's own Baron Munchausen

For those not in the know, Munchausen was a German baron made famous for his elaborate tails of travel and adventure. According to the fables, his feats included riding cannonballs travelling to the Moon, and escaping from a swamp by pulling himself up by his own hair.

Now, *The Companion* has unearthed equal exoticism with the life and times of one Sir Edward Wynter. How's single-handedly killing a tiger and defeating forty Arabs while on horse-back for starters? You can get a small snippet of Wytner's colourful life by visiting his grave at St Mary's Church, situated on the banks of the Thames on Battersea Church Road. His monument is just as elaborate as his life. It is located in the south gallery where a curious epitaph gives his exploits through life as an East India merchant. On the top is his bust, complete with whiskers, while his inscription lies underneath representing him in the act of performing the two exploits.

Born to be great in fortune as in mind, Too great to be within an isle confin'd; Young, helpless, friendless, seas unknown he tried; But English courage all those wants supplied. A pregnant wit, a painful diligence, Care to provide, and bounty to dispense; Join'd to a soul sincere, plain, open, just, Procur'd him friends, and friends procur'd him trust: These were his fortunè's rise, and thus began This hardy youth, rais'd to that happy man. A rare example, and unknown to the most Where wealth is gain'd, and conscience is not lost: Nor less in martial honor was his name, Witness his actions of immortal fame: Alone unarm'd, a tyger he oppress'd, And crush'd to death the monster of a beast. Twice twenty mounted Moors he overthrew Singly on foot, some wounded, some he flew, Dispers'd the rest,—what more could Sampson do? True to his friends, a terror to his foes, Here now in peace his honor'd bones repose!

His tales sound slightly shady and, as such, his life is hard to trace. But there is more. In 1585, he captained the ship *Aid* as part of Sir Francis Drake's fleet to Cartagena, situated on the South American coast, and where the English infantry captured the city and returned with Spanish loot. The fleet remained on the coast for six weeks of repair before sailing around Cuba, through the Florida Straits, and on to St Augustine as part of Drake's travels to the New World. As far as Wynter was concerned, his life continued to be as colourful as the places he visited under Drake's command. He was once captured at sea while travelling to France and exchanged for one Don Pedro de Faldas, who was a prisoner of the English. He succeeded his father as Lord of the Manor at Lydney in Gloucestershire. He was knighted by Queen Elizabeth at Greenwich on 18 June 1595, and became High Sheriff of Gloucestershire and a Knight of the Garter in the same year. For the last thirteen years of his life he lived at York House in Battersea and died aged sixty-four in 1686.

Sleep easy

It's not just Wandsworth residents who have got on the health bandwagon in the last few years. Her Majesty's finest have been requesting the herbals since 2001. Prisoners are relying on herbal tea rather than sedatives to calm themselves down as staff increase the peace by dishing out cups of the stuff. The prison pharmacy introduced Dr Stuart's Botanical Teas and word spread to other county prisons with names such as Tranquility and Valerian Plus.

Marks and spies

The unsuspecting shopper down St John's Road – that orange road with shops in Clapham Junction – would have had little idea as to the covert operations going on in the 1970s. Situated just off the borough's busiest shopping road, an MI5 operation was blown wide open by Russian spies after it was discovered that they had been secretly photographing them. Known as 'A4' agents (MI5 agents working in Section 4 of 'A' technical branch) and nicknamed 'The Watchers', their job was to observe their targets in specially equipped vehicles. As such, they needed a base to keep their goods and a garage on Barnard Road was deemed the perfect place. It has since been demolished and replaced by houses built next to the Marks & Spencers goods entrance.

Borough spy files

Five years before the outbreak of the First World War, both Britain and Germany were locked in a naval arms race to decipher which of the two fleets had the better technological advantage. It was a key time and the Committee of Imperial Defence enhanced its defence strategies by focusing on ways to combat German spies from Britain's naval ports. The media immediately began to hype up the news and even offered readers money in exchange for information on anyone looking like a German agent. On 22 February 1914, Frederick and Maud Gould were arrested on suspicion of espionage. Maud Gould was found in possession of sensitive documents relating to the Royal Navy, which she was carrying onto a train bound from Charing Cross Station in London to Ostend in Belgium. Her German-born husband Frederick was subsequently arrested at his home in Wandsworth. A considerable quantity of other stolen official documents was discovered there. The documents revealed that Frederick Gould had acted as a German spy for several years. He had regularly corresponded with a 'Mr St.' in Potsdam – in reality, the German spymaster

Gustav Steinhauer – and had asked for money in exchange for sensitive documents. Gould pleaded guilty and was sentenced to six years' penal servitude (imprisonment and hard labour) followed by deportation. His wife was found not guilty after the court found that there was insufficient evidence that she knew the contents of the documents that she was carrying.

MI5 files

File ref KV 2/2260

This heavily weeded file covering 1941-1944 dealt with investigations carried out into the LARK Organisation, the Secret Operations Executive circuit based at Trondheim in Norway between February and December 1942. It fell under suspicion when one of its leading members, Herluf Nygaard, returned to Britain having escaped from Gestapo hands in questionable circumstances. Nygaard and many of his colleagues passed through the Royal Victoria Patriotic School (RVPS) – that large Gothic-looking building off Trinity Road and already mentioned in *The Companion* – the MI9 centre which screened refugees and escapees arriving in the UK during the war. The file includes copies of Nygaard's own report of his escape, and the RVPS interrogation reports on Nygaard and Øiving Sørlie. Photographs are also included of Nygaard and his colleagues Arthur Pevik, Johnny Pevik, Olaf Strom and Sørlie, and there are various other items of correspondence relating to the case, including consideration of the list obtained by British agents in Sweden of Trondheim residents granted an extra wine ration, which included Nygaard's name and therefore raised great suspicion.

Clapham Junction,
Platform 10, 7.53 to Waterloo

The 'man on the Clapham omnibus' is a descriptive formulation of a reasonably educated and intelligent but non-specialist person – a reasonable man, a hypothetical person against whom a defendant's conduct might be judged in an English law civil action for negligence.

It is derived from the phrase 'the bald-headed man at the back of the Clapham omnibus', coined by the nineteenth-century journalist Walter Bagehot to describe the normal man of the City, and used because Clapham was seen to represent an ordinary part of London. In Australia, the expression is replaced by the 'man on the Bondi tram'.

An odorous borough

In the 1870s, Battersea had one of the few surviving marshy areas in Central London. It was thought to be unhealthy, because of the bad odours that emanated from the marsh, to be unsightly, because it was neither neat nor tidy, and to be socially undesirable, because licentious public fairs took place, with singing and dancing. To the Victorians it was a very unplace. Excavated material was brought in and the land 'reclaimed' for Battersea Park and for housing.

It remains a good example of the shortcomings of survey-based, problem-solving design. For what was 'the problem' at Battersea? To 'reclaim the marshlands', to 'improve an unsightly view', to 'discourage licentious behaviour', to 'improve the value of the surrounding houses', to 'dispose of the excavated material from the dock excavations', or to 'create a recreational facility'?

1852: Craig's telescope

No doubt there have been many strange occurrences on Wandsworth Common over the years, but one that must have stood out was the world's biggest refracting telescope that once stood there. It was the brainchild of Reverend Mr John Craig, although critics derided his invention as an 'expensive failure'. Archaeologists have attempted to find remains of the telescope over the years to disprove this theory. Craig, although not part of any astrological society or body, set out to answer two theories – did the planet Venus possess a moon, and to confirm the existence of Saturn's Crepe Ring. Those theories were never proved but Craig's intuition can't be ruled out. The site lies in the south west corner of the Common. The Common's northern boundary is defined by the public path that runs just south of the gardens of the houses in Routh Road. The western side stops on the grass verge pavement in Lyford Road.

Wandsworth's – make that London's – finest restaurant

The Ivy's nine-year run as London's favourite restaurant – and to the celebrity – ended in 2005 when the 8,000 reviewers for Harden's London Restaurant Guide preferred Chez Bruce, which caters for a more local clientele on the Bellevue Road. In the late Eighties the venue was called Harvey's, with Marco Pierre White causing havoc and winning accolades as chef. Nigel Platts-Martin, the owner, then installed Bruce Poole in the kitchen and in 1999 won a Michelin star.

From *Time Out*'s review guide:

This Wandsworth institution has an air of exclusivity. We booked several weeks ahead for two and still only managed an early sitting (6.30 p.m.). The first of the eponymous Bruce Poole's three impressive restaurants – the others are La Trompette and the Glasshouse – Chez Bruce combines outstanding food with a mildly subdued, reverential feel. It was quietly enjoyed, when we visited, by an almost uniform crowd of young professionals still in their suits. The best seats are near the window, while the main dining area behind can seem slightly airless (not helped by the lack of any focal point). We were delighted with everything the professional staff brought us. Rabbit came in various ways (terrine, rillettes, rolled breast, along with seared prunes and baked shallots): all full of flavour and the whole thing a visual treat. Venison loin (£4 supplement) was deliciously tender, with caramelised and mashed pear, while a pig's trotter, golden as a duck in Chinatown, was stuffed with a pleasingly rich mousse and chopped ham. Vanilla cheesecake came with pink rhubarb strips and mandarin sorbet: sharply impressive. There's a busy, knowledgeable sommelier to help you make the most of the highly regarded wine list. We love the fact that Chez Bruce takes its food so seriously, but we'd prefer a less serious atmosphere.

Walking the aisle

The mundane aspects offered by supermarkets is nothing compared to Sainsbury's on Clapham High Street. For those who know the history behind its current location, how many transport themselves back in time when walking down the frozen section? Transport is certainly the word, for it was previously a tram depot, a cinema, a bus garage, a museum, a bus garage again and a go-kart track. A horse tram depot was constructed in 1885, which was then converted for electric trams nineteen years later. The Globe Cinema was also based here from 1910 for five years. The war left the sheds badly damaged and they were rebuilt as a bus garages in 1950. In 1960 it became the Museum of British Transport until 1973. Up until 1996, the location was an indoor go-kart track, until Sainsbury's moved in.

Three from Gumtree

Gumtree is one of London's most popular web destinations for classified ads. Here are three messages from its popular 'Missed connections' section:

No. 345 bus, Clapham

> You asked me how far it was to Clapham junction if you walked, and I suggested you take the bus, we got on the 345 together, I got off at the stop before you. I felt we had a connection as you looked at me as the bus drove off. Would love to see you again.

Norbiton to Clapham

> You are late 20s to mid-30s with Billy Ray Cyrus hair, long and dark brown. I see you often at Norbiton and have fancied you for more or a less a year but im too shy to smile. I'm 25 on Tuesday , I used to have very long naturally mousey brown hair, now its very short dark hair and I wear dark glasses. Know me? Is it u? Get in touch.......x

Balham High Road

Girl crossing road, me in big red fire engine

You were crossing the road and looked into the cab. We
caught eyes and you were wondering why I wasn't dressed
in a fireman's outfit. I then opened the window and told
you my house had burnt down and I wasn't actually a
fireman. You laughed briefly before smiling and crossing
the road. Wish I could meet you again and tell you that
even though I felt awful because my house had just burnt
down, I felt even worse when you laughed at my burnt
down house.

Clapham's rail disaster

20 December 2008 marked twenty years since the fatal
Clapham Junction rail disaster when thirty-five people died
after three trains were involved in a collision during morning
rush hour on the line between Wandsworth Common and
the Junction. Two commuter trains, carrying an estimated
1,300 passengers between them, collided shortly after
8 a.m., while a third empty train later ran into the wreckage
killing some passengers who had survived the first crash.
The accident took place when the 07:18 from Basingstoke
to Waterloo approached the Junction.

Reports indicate it was slowing for signals when the
06:14 from Poole, travelling from Bournemouth due to
track problems, ran into the back of it. It was viewed as the
worst train accident of recent times. The Hidden inquiry
into the Clapham crash reported that the primary cause
was 'wiring errors' made by a rail worker who had had
one day off in thirteen weeks. British Rail work practices
were also to blame and the inquiry made ninety-three

recommendations for safety improvements, including a limit on the hours signalmen were allowed to work.

Putney to Portsmouth pub banter

It's 1792 and France is leading the way with a breakthrough signalling system by using towers ten miles apart to send messages hundreds of miles at around 1.75 words per minute.

With the Napoleonic War looming, the Royal Navy Headquarters – the Admiralty – in London began to take note as it looked to find the quickest way possible to send messages between the capital and Portsmouth. Horseback was the quickest at a shade under five hours.

The Admiralty came upon a design by Reverend Lord George Murray Each where a series of stations used a system of shutters, which could be raised or lowered according to a code. Experimental trials were carried out on Wimbledon Common in 1795 and its success saw Murray awarded £2,000 for his invention. The stations were:

1   Roof of the first Lord's house – Whitehall
2   Chelsea – Royal Hospital
3   Putney – near Telegraph Inn pub
4   Cabbage Hill – near Chessington Zoo
5   Netley Heath – 'Telegraph', Blind Oak Gate
6   Hascombe – Telegraph Hill
7   Blackdown – Tally Knob
8   Beacon Hill – Harting Down
9   Portsdown Hill – various references, such as 'Cosham Road Junction – south of crossroads', 'near Cliffdene Cottage'
10   Portsmouth – Southsea Common by Clarence Pier

On a clear day, a message could be transmitted from London to Portsmouth in around fifteen minutes. On a foggy day, it was somewhat different. Here, Putney played a crucial role as the London fog meant that messages couldn't be received in Chelsea. It was then a case of running to deliver the message.

There were probably four men at each station. Two men watched through telescopes and when they saw the signal 'all shutters closed' or 123456, two 'ropemen' would then operate the station's shutters to the next station. On 18 May 1814 peace was proclaimed and Napoleon banished to the Isle of Elba. A year later he had escaped and England was again at war with the telegraphs back up and running. Seven weeks later Napoleon was defeated at Waterloo and the Admiralty announced plans to establish a series of stations using Semaphore – a machine with moveable arms that give visual signals. Putney's telegraph closed on 31 December 1847, with its last superintendent as Lieutenant Lardner Dennys – a veteran of the Battle of Trafalgar. It is still unknown whether Dennys was behind the birth of the pub.

A wheel keeps on turning

Wandsworth Common Windmill, a conserved Grade II listed smock mill that lies off Spencer Park, was built in 1837 to drain water from the railway cutting of the London and Southampton Railway. The water was pumped into an ornamental lake on Wandsworth Common which had been dug by Mr Wilson, the founder of Price's Candle Works. The mill was working c.1870, but the lake was drained and filled in in 1884. The mill then lost its purpose and ceased work, with the sails removed. The remains can still be seen today by the railway cutting at Spencer Park by Trinity

Road. When the railway was built in the 1830s, it was feared that the cutting would be flooded by water from a large pond nearby, known as the Black Sea. The railway company provided the windmill to pump waters from the cutting back to the pond.

Twentieth-century boy

What? Marc Bolan's shrine.

Where? Queens Ride, off Upper Richmond Road, Putney.

In the early 1970s, Marc Bolan and his band T-Rex became the biggest thing since the Beatles. They notched up ten top five UK singles, sold millions of records and were known for top hits such as 'Hot Love', 'Get It On', 'Telegram Sam' and '20th Century Boy'.

However, on 16 September 1977, tragedy struck when Bolan's purple Mini crashed into a tree near Putney Common, killing him and badly injuring his partner, Gloria Jones, who had been driving the car. Within hours, his flat had been broken into and important documents stolen. Despite T-Rex having sold close to 40 million records, Bolan's estate was worth a paltry £10,000 – his missing fortune remaining a mystery to this day. 'The Bolan Tree' is officially recognised by The English Tourist Board as 'Marc Bolan's Rock Shrine' in their Guide *England Rocks*. In 1998, the press reported that 'the Bolan Tree', had 'less than three years' before it would have to be felled. It resulted in the formation of the T-Rex Action Group (TAG) in 1999.

Celeb watch

In today's celeb-obsessed world, *The Companion* has succumbed to revealing local celebrity residents:

Alun Armstrong – actor,
Marcus Brigstocke – comedian
Jack Dee – comedian/actor
Sophie Dahl – model
Jason Flemyng – actor
Mark Owen – singer
Ainsley Harriott – television chef
Kiera Knightley – actress
Gordon Ramsay – chef
Prunella Scales – actor
Dana International – Israeli winner of the Eurovision Song Contest
Johnny Vaughan – television presenter
Phil Spencer – television
Kevin Pietersen – England cricket player
Holly Willoughby – television presenter

Wandsworth Prison

Charles Bronson, one of Britain's most notorious inmates, said that Wandsworth Prison is one of the toughest jails he has ever been in. In a self-penned book, he wrote, 'Everyone loves Wanno – I don't think so. I've had more kickings in there than I care to remember.'

And in another paragraph that makes you want to stay on the straight and narrow at all costs, he said: 'I would arrive naked in a body belt and the treatment would kick

George Davey was sentenced to one month's hard labour in Wandsworth Prison in 1872 for stealing two rabbits. He was just ten years old.

off from one. These blocks were run by a fist of steel. Always the biggest and ugliest screws in the jail. Not one under 6ft.'

The Companion says:

> ... that Bronson has served more than 30 years in more than
> 100 jails in the UK, and has spent much of that time in
> solitary confinement. Originally convicted for his part in
> an armed robbery in 1974, Bronson was sentenced to seven
> years but has had his term extended repeatedly. He has
> staged rooftop protests and held a prison teacher hostage,
> reportedly demanding a helicopter to Cuba and a cheese
> and pickle sandwich. Bronson changed his name after a bare
> knuckle fight promoter said it would be a bigger pull than
> his real name, Michael Peters.

The most important clothing of all...

Can Wandsworth lay claim to this title? For this we will
have to go into Wandsworth Plain, close to the Crane
Pub – reputedly one of the borough's oldest pubs – and
on to Church Row. Past a row of eighteenth-century
houses, which were built for prosperous merchants, stood
Middle Mill, which in the sixteenth century produced a
scarlet dye. This colour was to make Wandsworth famous
throughout Europe. It was the colour used by the Vatican's
cardinals and it is believed that it favoured Wandsworth's
dye to any other.

Water way to go to work

It not only provides a much-needed transport link for residents living at Wandsworth's waterfront developments, but it also marks a contrasting way into work for the masses. The River Taxi has always been in the thoughts of *The Companion* as a relaxing way to start the day. But so far it has been saved for a day off, for a trip into town. The route goes as follows:

Putney-Wandsworth Riverside-Chelsea Harbour-Cadogan Pier-Embankment-Blackfriars and runs from 06:20 to 07:10. The fastest journey to Blackfriars is thirty-five minutes.

Targets

People are five times more likely to become victims of identity fraud if they live in one of London's affluent areas – and Wandsworth is top of the list. According to figures, identity crime had soared 66 per cent in a year in 2008, as criminals looked to target the capital's most sought-after postcodes. Kensington, Richmond-upon-Thames, Putney, Wimbledon and the Kings Road were all obvious areas. But most at risk of all was the SW17 6 postal code, which centres on College Gardens in Tooting.

Five power station facts

In 2004, Battersea Power Station was on the New York-based World Monument Fund's List of 100 Most Endangered Sites, which includes Angkor Wat in Cambodia, sites on Easter Island and the Temple of Hercules in Rome.

Battersea Power Station in all its glory.

Sir Giles Gilbert Scott was enlisted as architect for the Power Station, which was opened in 1937. Scott was famous for designing the classic red telephone box.

The Power Station has held mass appeal from music artists over the years. The iconic four towers have featured on albums by the Orb, Pink Floyd, The Who and Morrissey.

The station also stood in for an Eastern European military camp in a MacGyver television movie, *The Lost Treasure of Atlantis*.

Many elaborate plans have been mooted since it closed in the 1980s. The Grade II listed building was sold to a property company in 2006 for £400 million. It remains to be seen what these companies actually decide to do with one of London's finest landmarks.

Bombed out

The local press come out with great stories on a regular basis and the *Wandsworth Guardian* is no different.

A farcical law designed to compensate people who were bombed out during the Second World War was last year used to force a council to buy a patch of grass which cost more than 100 times its market value. Taxpayers were looking at footing a bill of around £1.6 million to buy a 0.22 acre plot from a property firm, despite its true value being £15,000.

The judge who ordered Wandsworth Council to pay the fee described the scenario as 'utterly deplorable'. The resulting win left fears of similar cases springing up across the London areas that were bombed by the Luftwaffe.

The dispute centred on a scrap of land upon which a row of Victorian terrace houses stood until they were destroyed by what is believed to have been a V1 flying bomb. After the war Wandsworth Council cleared the site and added it to Fred Wells Gardens, a neighbouring public park in Battersea.

The land, however, was privately owned and was bought for £30,000 in 2001 by an investment firm that wanted to build houses there. When the borough refused planning permission, the company served a purchase notice compelling Wandsworth to purchase the land because it would not allow access for any commercial purpose.

The property firm's legal team invoked an offbeat clause in the Land Compensation Act 1961 which gave automatic planning permission for the rebuilding of houses destroyed by German bombs. It meant the value of the land suddenly rose to £1.6million.

Name and shame

Wandsworth Borough is no place for the owners of pets who foul the footpath. In November 1996, the Tory council introduced a policy of `naming and shaming' any of its tenants found guilty of anti-social behaviour. The first batch of miscreants to have their crimes publicised included twenty-three such dog-owners, three residents guilty of noise pollution and four families who had been deemed to be 'bad neighbours'.

Spies, gallows and treason

During the Second World War, Wandsworth Prison played host to some of the most infamous spies and traitors in the country, leaving another colourful episode in the times of the borough's famous jail.

In the sixty years up to the beginning of the war in which HMP Wandsworth's gallows had been open for business, sixty-nine executions had been carried out.

That number was set to increase sharply with the arrival of some of the country's most infamous spies and traitors. The group was made up of those with alleged Nazi sympathies or a cause of trouble if left at liberty. This included Germans, and other nationalities, including British, as well as members of the IRA.

On 23 May 1940, an Act of Parliament was passed to allow civilian courts to try people for spying as a way of increasing the scope of the death penalty. One prisoner received in the prison at that time was George Owens. The prison's first spy, he was held in the prison as a double agent after feeding misinformation to the Germans.

At the same time, Wandsworth was the focus of more and more frequent air raids. In September 1940, the prison suffered its first war damage – an anti-aircraft shell landing in the photography studio. The Governor at the time, Major B.D. Grew, made the following note in the prison records:

9 September: Night of Bombing

10 September: Night of indiscriminate bombing

12 September: All night raid – heavy AA (anti Aircraft) bombs nearby. No damage to prison

20 September: Bomber brought down after direct hit – back of prison

28 September: 10 bombs dropped inside prison. Smashed A wing, RC Chapel, Old Hospital, PWS incendiary bombs dropped, put out

11 October: Six incendiary bombs in prison, many incendiary bombs in quarters put out. Two quarters damaged.

In November, Wandsworth held its first spy to face execution under the Treachery Act. Dutchman Charles Van der Kieboom landed on British shores with fellow countryman Sjoerd Pons with radio equipment and code signals. After being sentenced to death, it is suggested, Pons turned Queen's evidence (Pons was found not guilty). Van der Kieboom claimed he had been forced to work for the Germans. His appeal failed and he was executed at Pentonville on 17 December 1940.

The first execution at the jail for treachery took place on 9 July 1941. The details are sketchy and only read 'Armstrong – In USA intent to assist the enemy.'

The first spies to be executed at Wandsworth were Karl Drucke and Werner Walti. They had come ashore from a Luftwaffe seaplane near Banff, Scotland. The pair separated and Walti was soon arrested carrying a radio, pistol and British currency. Drucke managed to get to Edinburgh before he too was arrested. With no use for either of them as double agents, they were tried and eventually executed on 6 August 1941.

Eight days later German Army Sergeant Joseph Jakobs was also executed, but under unique circumstances. Caught parachuting into Britain and badly breaking his ankle on landing, he was found guilty of espionage. On the morning of 14 August 1941, he was transported to the Tower of London to be executed by firing squad. Major Grew remembered Jakobs shaking his hand and thanking him for the consideration given to him in prison. Still in pain from his broken ankle, he managed to click his heals and salute before finding a place in history as the last person to be executed at the Tower.

There was no such dignified end for the next spy held at Wandsworth. Karl Richter, a Sudeten German in origin, went to the gallows on 10 December 1941 with a considerable struggle. Like previous spies, he had parachuted into England where his unhelpful and abrupt manner to a lorry driver had his behaviour reported to the police, who subsequently detained him. He apparently tried to knock himself unconscious in the cell but when this failed he struggled desperately, breaking the leather strap which was securing his wrists.

The first British subject to be executed at the prison was Jose Estella Key. He had reported shipping movements from 'the Rock' (Gibraltar) and was brought to Britain for interrogation and trial. He was executed at a double execution on 7 July 1942 alongside Alphonse Timmerman, a Belgian who came to England posing as a refugee but found guilty of treachery.

The last spy to be executed at Wandsworth was Fransiscus Winter. Like others before, he tried the refugee angle as part of his defence but to no avail. He went to his death on 26 January 1943.

The Wandsworth gallows would claim two more under the Treason Act – both high profile.

Firstly, Jon Amery was executed on 19 December 1945. He had supported the German cause, making radio broadcasts and getting British prisoners of war to form a small unit of the German Army. He was the son of a Cabinet minister, Sir Leo Amery, and the elder brother of Julian Amery. Julian later served his country in the army and went on to become an MP and was elevated to the peerage. The execution was one of the few recalled by executioner Albert Pierrepoint, with Amery greeting him and the two exchanging pleasantries.

The last execution for treason was the most famous. William Joyce – more commonly known as Lord Haw Haw because of his nasal drawl – broadcast radio propaganda against Britain throughout the war. Although born in the USA, he had previously declared himself Irish (prior to partition) and thereby entitled to British citizenship and a British passport.

(Based on Stuart McLaughlin's book on Wandsworth. *Exectution Suite*).

A champion runner

We have already mentioned Wandsworth's celebrated Olympic runner, Albert Hill. But less well-known is John Levett, a nineteenth-century athlete and twice champion runner of England. Born in 1826, Levett lived with his parents in New Road, Battersea and he was soon training at Garratt Lane. By 1851 he was running ten miles in under fifty-two minutes and the following year he had picked up his second Champion Runner of England title.

It was after this second title that a series of races came about to determine the best athlete over the hour mark. It brought about a string of thrilling races, as well as wages, as Levett travelled the country. After one such race in Liverpool in 1864, two men approached Levett looking for a man to run eleven miles in one hour on the first race day, followed by twenty miles in two hours the following day. It was a mammoth feat even by Levett's high standards, but the Wandsworth man took up the offer and he was soon training at Hoylake and Aintree racecourses. Levett ran eleven miles in fifty-eight minutes on the first race at Rock Ferry, but the following day he was clearly struggling and was forced to give up after an hour and twenty-nine minutes, completing fifteen and a half miles.

A year later Levett was back on his home patch. A series of races ensued against James Pudney, a rival from Mile End who also held the Champion Runner belt at the time. Levett won the first six-miler in a topsy-turvy race close to Garratt Lane and a re-match was marked for the following month. In May 1855 there was a re-run at Wandsworth over six miles and this time Pudney came out on top in a thrilling climax. In 1857 he was back at Garratt Lane, but a local report noted that an overweight Levett perhaps contributed to a heavy defeat.

By now Levett had taken up roles managing running tracks and in 1860 he was listed as owner of a Dublin track, the Rotunda. It was here that Levett challenged a Red Indian called Deerfoot to a ten mile race. 6,000 spectators whipped up a typical Irish atmosphere at the track and they

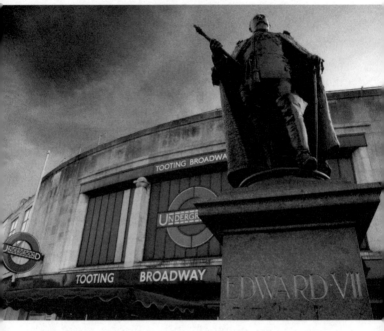

Wandsworth's only statue of any note, King Edward VII.

were treated to a fine race for much of the early part. Levett, however, soon retired after five miles but Deerfoot kept on going and finished in fifty-two minutes.

Lonely statue

When *The Companion* treks north over the Thames, it is immediately met with a plethora of statues on the Chelsea side. A sign of wealth and prosperity in remembrance of those that lived there perhaps, but what about statues in

Wandsworth? Unless it is very much mistaken, the only statue of any note is the one of Edward VII outside Tooting Broadway station. Erected on the corner in 1911, Edward is posing as Commander in Chief and was sculpted by one of the most prolific artists of war memorials, L.F. Roslyn, who saw service in the Royal Flying Corps.

Born on 9 November 1841, Edward was a popular monarch but had to wait until he was almost sixty, being the first born of Queen Victoria, before he came to the throne in 1901. During his reign, Edward was a mischievous King as far as his indiscretions with women were concerned, and following his death in 1910 after a bout of bronchitis, he left his wife Alexandra, six children and a string of mistresses in his wake.

Party time

The National Tennis Centre in Roehampton states on its website that it is the 'focal point for Britain's top players'. They certainly have got that right – but not all for the right reasons. While Laura Robson continues to show British tennis fans that there might be life after Jo Durie after all, other up-and-coming players have not faired so well in the spotlight.

Perhaps it's the spotlight they don't crave, as most of the headlines coming out of the NTC seem to be related to evening activities. No sooner had the £30 million centre opened in 2007 than two emerging talents had their money halted. It came after David Rice, eighteen, the second-ranked boy in Britain, and seventeen-year-old Naomi Broady, the Girls' 18-and-Under national champion, posted photographs of themselves on a social-networking site showing their indulgences towards junk food and alcohol. And last year one leading junior was hit with a record suspension for staying out until the early hours on the very day of a doubles match – the second round at Wimbledon. Dan Evans, the British junior No. 3, was stripped of all funding and support by the Lawn Tennis Association for four months. If that was bad enough, he had earlier been spotted on CCTV cameras returning to the NTC at 4 a.m. after a one-sided defeat at Queen's by Belgium's Xavier Malisse. Just to make up the foursome, his Wimbledon partner Daniel Smethurst was hit by a similar penalty, but only for two months as he had a good character.

Putney debates

The battle of ideas which took place at Putney Church in October 1647 profoundly influenced British politics for the next 350 years. Here, thoughts emerged which still influence our lives today; ideas took hold which led men to demand a say over their future. They wanted control over their politics and communities – how their money was spent and accountability from those in power. It was here that democratic socialism was born – the right of the lowliest individual to have a say in the shape of their society. It was the start of a process that would end in votes for all and the democracy of the Westminster Parliament.

A brewing master

By far the oldest and longest serving chairman in the British brewing industry, John Young, died in September 2006 in the same week that London's oldest brewery ended more than 400 years of brewing at its Wandsworth site. Young was buried on the same day that the Ram Brewery closed its doors for the last time. Here is his obituary, written by prominent beer writer Roger Protz, to give an understanding how important Young was to the industry and to Wandsworth.

John Young, who has died aged eighty-five, will have a prominent place in the Brewers' Hall of Fame, revered as the father of the 'real ale revolution', an iconoclast who believed in good traditional beer drunk in good traditional pubs. Young, chairman of Young's of Wandsworth in south London for forty-four years, steered the family brewery on a different course from the rest of the industry in the 1970s. It was a course that was derided at the time: however, it proved not only successful for Young's but also encouraged other regional brewers to follow suit.

A spate of mergers in the 1960s had created six national brewers who attempted to transform the way beer was made by switching from cask ale to keg beer – filtered, pasteurised and artificially carbonated. Panic ensued as such brands as Watney's Red Barrel, Worthington E and Whitbread Tankard rapidly dominated the market. Smaller regional brewers rushed to emulate the 'Big Six', as they were known.

In Wandsworth, John Young raised his standard above the Ram Brewery, on the oldest brewing site in Britain, and declared he would remain faithful to beer that matured naturally in its cask. He was laughed to scorn by directors of other breweries. Among the legion of stories about him, one is told of a meeting of the Brewers' Society in London where, during a break for coffee, one member saw a funeral hearse passing by outside. 'There goes another of your customers, John,' he told Young, to roars of laughter from his colleagues. John Young had the last laugh.

He was born in Winchester, the eldest of four sons of William Allen Young. The family was steeped in brewing. John was the great-great-grandson of Charles Allen Young, one of two businessmen who took over the sixteenth-century Ram Brewery in 1831. John's mother was Joan Barrow Simonds, a member of the family that owned Simonds Brewery in Reading.

But John's first love was sailing: he was educated at the Nautical College in Pangbourne. Sailing holidays in the late 1930s on the river Orwell in Suffolk brought John and his brothers into contact with Arthur Ransome at Pin Mill, the setting for *We Didn't Mean to Go to Sea*. Ransome claimed that he, rather than the brothers' father, introduced the boys to the pleasures of beer and darts.

Either side of the Second World War, John went to Corpus Christi College, Cambridge, where he graduated with an honours degree in economics. During the war he served with distinction as a fighter pilot on aircraft carriers. He left the Fleet Air Arm as a Lieutenant Commander in 1947 and launched a career in shipping. For a while he was based in Antwerp, where he met his Belgian wife Yvonne. They married in 1951 and settled in West Sussex, from where John, with his brothers, was summoned to work at the Ram Brewery in 1954.

He succeeded his father as chairman in 1962 and set about refashioning the company to meet the challenges of the time. Improving the pub estate and offering children's

We've been round
the bend since 1831

YOUNG'S

The Ram Brewery Wandsworth

Young's Brewery sign.

rooms – a daring move at the time – did not mean a move away from traditional values. The brewery retained a fierce commitment to cask beer and delivered it to local pubs by horse-drawn drays, while a live ram mascot, along with ducks and geese, were familiar if bizarre sights at Wandsworth.

The energetic new chairman visited every pub in his estate. He was on first name terms with his landlords and became friendly with regular customers. Company annual general meetings became lavish affairs where a white-suited

John Young would proclaim his belief in traditional brewing values. He was so horrified by the way some London pubs were being remodelled in the 1970s – as Wild West saloons or sputniks – that he once threatened to enter one pub armed with a packet of soap flakes to throw into a large fountain that had been installed there.

The commitment to cask beer paid off. Sales of Young's ales rocketed and their success was instrumental in helping the Campaign for Real Ale to make its mark in the early 1970s. In 1975 John Young was made a CBE to mark his work in brewing and for charity: he was chairman of the National Hospital for Nervous Diseases in Bloomsbury and raised millions of pounds to build new wards and install modern equipment.

His passion for brewing remained unabated, and John continued to work and chair company AGMs up to this year, though he was visibly ill with cancer. His last few months in office were dogged by controversy: a redevelopment scheme in Wandsworth meant the brewery had to close. When a suitable alternative site could not be found in London, Young's agreed to merge its brewing operations with Charles Wells of Bedford, a move that has not pleased all lovers of Young's distinctive beers.

But 200 Young's pubs will remain in London and the south-east, bricks and mortar reminders of the man who guided their fortunes with undiminished fervour for more than forty years.

And finally…

Zodiac Records, that record shop on the corner of Old York Road close to the Wandsworth roundabout and the bottom of East Hill. Has anyone ever been in and is it really open on Saturdays? Email *The Companion* at wandsworthcompanion.com.

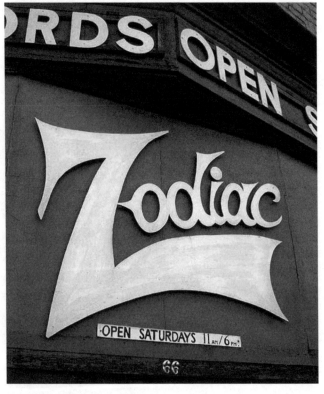

Zodiac Records, Wandsworth.